FAT-FREE BAKING

Scrumptious Cakes, Cookies, Brownies, Pies, Muffins, Breads, & Other Goodies

SANDRA WOODRUFF, RD

Avery Publishing Group

Garden City Park, New York

Text Illustrator: John Wincek
Interior Color Photographs: John Harper
Cover Photograph: Envision/Steven Mark Needham
Cover Design: William Gonzalez
Typesetting: Baker & Baker/John and Rhonda Wincek
In-House Editor: Joanne Abrams

Cataloging-in-Publication Data

Woodruff, Sandra L.
    Fat-free baking: scrumptious cakes, cookies, brownies, pies, muffins, breads and other goodies / Sandra Woodruff
        p. cm
        ISBN 0-89529-630-6

    1. Baking. 2. Lowfat diet recipes. I. Title.
TX765.W66 1994   641.8′15dc20

Copyright © 1994 by Sandra Woodruff

Printed in the United States of America

10 9 8 7 6 5 4 3 2 1

FAT-FREE BAKING

Contents

This book is dedicated to my favorite taste tester, Wiley Coyote.

Acknowledgments

So many people have been constant sources of inspiration, ideas, and information that it is hard to know where to begin these acknowledgments.

I would like to thank Rudy Shur and Avery Publishing Group for the opportunity to publish this book. I am also grateful to my editor, Joanne Abrams, whose efforts have added so much to this book and who, like everyone at Avery, has been a pleasure to work with.

My sincere gratitude also goes to the following people who have been especially supportive: My very significant other, Tom Maureau, my mother, Wanda Burlison; my father and stepmother, George and Jeanne Woodruff; and my dear friends, Gail Bauman, Lori Turner, Toni Trimarco, Robert Baker, Lisa Harris, and Sara Goldiner. Thanks also go to my colleagues at Tallahassee Community Hospital's Communicare Center—the most enthusiastic and supportive group of co-workers anyone could ask for.

A special thanks goes to Ellie Whitney, PhD, and Mary Jo Weale, PhD, for their patience and kindness, and for teaching me so much.

As a nutritionist, I have long been aware of the need to help people eliminate fat from their diets. I also know the importance of creating nutrient-rich foods made with whole grains and other ingredients that are as close as possible to their natural state. And from years of working with people, I know that foods must be more than just healthy. They must look appetizing and taste delicious. If not, people simply won't eat them.

Fat-Free Baking is the perfect book for people who want to reduce the fat in their diet, maximize their nutrition, and still enjoy great-tasting sweet treats. From Strawberry Streusel Muffins, to Peach Pizzaz Pie, to Colossal Chocolate Chippers, to Fresh Apple Cake, every recipe has been designed to eliminate or greatly reduce fat, and to boost nutrition. Just as important, every recipe has been kitchen-tested to make sure that you enjoy success each and every time you make it, and people-tested to make sure that every treat you create is sure to be a hit.

The first chapter of *Fat-Free Baking* begins by explaining just why dietary fat should be reduced, and just how much fat is allowable in a healthy diet. It also provides information about a variety of whole grain flours and less-refined sweeteners that will help you maximize nutrition in all your cooking.

Chapters 2 through 6 each focus on one type of fat substitute and present a fabulous selection of recipes for delicious fat-free baked goods made with that substitute. Each chapter also guides you in using that substitute to create fat-free versions of your own favorite recipes. You will discover just how fruit juices and purées; nonfat yogurt and buttermilk; liquid sweeteners; prunes; and sweet potatoes, pumpkins, and other squashes can replace the fat in baked goods. The result? Super-moist and delicious quick breads, muffins, cakes, cookies, pies, and other treats made with absolutely no butter, margarine, or oil!

The last chapter of the book shows you how to use reduced-fat margarine and light butter to make lower-fat baked goods. (Yes, these ingredients can be used in baking!) These substitutes reduce the fat in baked goods by more than 50 percent, and are wonderful products for people who are used to baking with traditional full-fat shortening, and are just beginning to reduce the fat in their diets.

It is my hope that *Fat-Free Baking* will prove to you, as well as to your friends and family, that baked goods do not have to be rich and fattening; that cakes, muffins, and other treats can provide nutritional value; and that fat-free and low-fat foods can be satisfying, exciting, and fun. I wish you the best of luck and health in all your cooking adventures!

aking and eating great food is one of life's simplest yet greatest pleasures. And for most people, home-baked goods top the list of favorite foods. Cookies fresh from the oven, bubbling cobblers and fruit crisps, hearty muffins and quick breads, and moist and delicious cakes warm the hearts of young and old alike. Homemade baked goods are also a special part of many family traditions, and treasured recipes are often passed from generation to generation with loving care. Just the aroma of freshly baked cookies, breads, and cakes can bring back memories of special times.

Until very recently, though, most baked goods were made with large amounts of butter, margarine, oil, and other high-fat ingredients—ingredients that we now know must be kept to a minimum in a healthy diet. The good news is that this awareness has led people to explore new ways of cooking and eating. As a result, many low-fat cookbooks are now available. But while these cookbooks do provide low-fat recipes, they often reduce fat and calories by using artificial fat substitutes and sweeteners. In the process, nutrition is often compromised. *Fat-Free Baking* is a very different kind of cookbook. It was designed to help you create delicious low- and no-fat baked goods that are also high in nutrition.

As a nutritionist and teacher—and as a person who loves good food—I began looking for ways to reduce or totally eliminate dietary fat long before anyone ever heard the term "fat-free." Through years of experimentation and kitchen testing, and with the help of clients and students, I have developed simple ways to make moist and flavorful breads, muffins, cakes, and cookies with little or no fat. I have also improved the nutritional value of baked goods by using natural sweeteners like fruits and juices whenever possible to reduce the need for added sugar. Whole grain flours have also been incorporated into these recipes, providing added fiber and extra nutritional value.

As you will see, eliminating the fat from baked goods is easy. The recipes in this book will help you use naturally nutritious ingredients like fruit purées and juices, nonfat yogurt and buttermilk, liquid sweeteners like molasses, prunes, and pumpkin and other squashes to replace the fats traditionally used in baking. The result? Super-moist and delicious quick breads, muffins, cakes, cookies, and other treats— with absolutely no butter, margarine, or oil. And for those who are not quite ready to give up all shortening, guidelines and recipes have been provided for baking with reduced-fat margarine and light butter. This decreases the fat in baked goods by more than 50 percent!

Besides being low in fat and high in nutrition, the recipes in *Fat-Free Baking* have an added feature: their simplicity. Every effort has been made to keep the number of ingredients to a minimum and to use as few bowls, pans, and utensils as possible. In fact, the vast majority of recipes are easily mixed by hand in one bowl, and are simple enough for beginners.

So even if you've never baked before, preheat the oven and get ready to have a great time. And get your kids involved too—this book is a wonderful way to introduce baking and healthful eating to children. Let this be the start of some new and delicious family traditions!

1 FAT-FREE BAKING AT ITS BEST

Sometimes you can have your cake and eat it too . . . and your bread, and your muffins, and your cookies. Who can resist moist and delicious homemade breads, muffins, cookies, and cakes—especially when they are fat-free, wholesome, and incredibly simple to make? This book presents recipes for a variety of baked goods that are totally fat-free or greatly reduced in fat. Experienced bakers and novices alike will be surprised by the number of creative and healthful ways in which fat can be replaced in baked goods.

This chapter will explain why dietary fat should be decreased, and will guide you in budgeting your daily fat intake. In addition, you will learn about the various healthful ingredients used throughout this book—ingredients that may be old friends of yours, or may become new additions to your pantry.

BIG FAT PROBLEMS

xcess fat may well be the number-one dietary problem in America. With more than twice the calories of carbohydrates and protein, fat is a concentrated source of calories. Compare a cup of butter or margarine (almost pure fat) with a cup of flour (almost pure carbohydrates). The butter has 1,600 calories, and the flour has 400 calories. If you look at the ingredients in a cookie recipe, the source of the greatest number of calories becomes very obvious.

Calorie and Fat Amounts in Sugar Cookie Ingredients		
Ingredient	Calories	Fat
2 cups flour	800	4.5 grams
1 cup sugar	720	0 grams
1 cup butter	1,600	177 grams
2 eggs	150	10 grams

Not only is fat high in calories, but it is also readily converted into body fat when eaten in excess. Carbohydrate-rich foods eaten in excess are also stored as fat, but they must first be converted into fat—a process that burns up some of the carbohydrates. The bottom line is that a high-fat diet will cause 20 percent more weight gain than will a high-carbohydrate diet, even when the two diets contain the same number of calories. So a high-fat diet is a double-edged sword for the weight-conscious person. It is high in calories, and it is high in the kind of nutrient that is most readily stored as body fat.

But high-fat diets pose a threat to much more than our weight. When fatty diets lead to obesity, diseases like diabetes and high blood pressure can result. And specific types of fats present their own unique problems. For example, eating too much saturated fat—found in butter, margarine, and other solid fats—raises blood cholesterol levels, setting the stage for heart disease.

Polyunsaturated fat, once thought to be the solution to heart disease, can also be harmful when eaten in excess. A diet overly rich in corn oil, safflower oil, and other foods high in polyunsaturates can alter body chemistry to favor the development of blood clots, high blood pressure, and inflammatory diseases. Too much polyunsaturated fat can also promote free-radical damage in cells, contributing to heart disease and cancer.

Where do monounsaturated fats fit in? Monounsaturated fats—found in olive oil, canola oil, avocados, and nuts—have no known harmful effects other than being a concentrated source of calories, as all fats are.

Considering the problems caused by excess fat, you may think that it would be best to totally eliminate fat from your diet. But the fact is that we do need some dietary fat. For instance, linoleic acid, a polyunsaturated fat naturally present in grains, nuts, and seeds, is essential for life. The average adult needs a minimum of 3 to 6 grams of linoleic acid per day—the amount present in 1 to 2 teaspoonfuls of polyunsaturated vegetable oil or 1 to 2 tablespoonfuls of nuts and seeds. Linolenic acid, a fat found mainly in fish and green plants, is also essential for good health.

Unfortunately, many people are getting too much of a good thing. The liberal use of foods like mayonnaise, oil-based salad dressings, margarine, and cooking oils has created an unhealthy overdose of linoleic acid in the American diet. And, of course, most people also eat far too much saturated fat. How can we correct this? We can minimize the use of refined vegetable oils and table fats, and eat a diet rich in whole grains and vegetables, with moderate amounts of nuts and seeds. This is what *Fat-Free Baking* is all about. In the next section, you'll learn how to budget your daily fat intake. Throughout the remainder of the book, you'll learn how to use healthful foods to prune the fat from your diet and maximize the nutrients.

BUDGETING YOUR FAT

For most people, close to 40 percent of the calories in their diet come from fat. However, currently it is recommended that fat calories constitute no more than 30 percent of the diet, and, in fact, 20 to 25 percent would be even better for most people. So the amount of fat you can eat every day is based on the number of calories you need. Because people's caloric needs depend on their weight, age, sex, activity level, and metabolic rate, these needs vary greatly among people. Most adults, though, must consume 13 to 15 calories per pound to maintain their weight. Of course, some people need even fewer calories, while very physically active people may need even more.

Once you have determined your calorie requirement, you can estimate a fat budget for yourself. Suppose you are a moderately active person who weighs 150 pounds. You will probably need about 15 calories per pound to maintain your weight, or about 2,250 calories per day. To limit your fat intake to 20 percent of your caloric intake, you can eat no more than 450 fat calories per day (2,250 x .20 = 450). To convert this into grams of fat, divide by 9, as one gram of fat has 9 calories. Therefore, you should limit yourself to 50 grams of fat per day (450 ÷ 9 = 50).

The following table shows both 20-percent and 25-percent maximum daily fat gram budgets. If you are overweight or underweight, go by the weight you would like to be. And keep in mind that although you have budgeted *X* amount of fat grams per day, you don't *have* to eat that amount of fat—you just have to avoid going over budget.

Maximum Daily Fat Intake			
Weight	Recommended Daily Calorie Intake (13–15 calories/pound)	Fat Grams Allowed (20%)	Fat Grams Allowed (25%)
100	1,300–1,500	29–33	36–42
110	1,430–1,650	32–37	40–46
120	1,560–1,800	34–40	43–50
130	1,690–1,950	38–43	47–54
140	1,820–2,100	40–46	51–58
150	1,950–2,250	43–50	54–62
160	2,080–2,400	46–53	58–67
170	2,210–2,550	49–57	61–71
180	2,340–2,700	52–60	65–75
190	2,470–2,850	55–63	69–79
200	2,600–3,000	58–66	72–83

ABOUT THE INGREDIENTS

good portion of the excess dietary fat in most people's diet comes from baked goods like cakes and cookies. Fat has traditionally been used to impart moistness and tenderness to these sweets. This book will show you how you can totally eliminate or dramatically reduce the fat content of your favorite treats by using more healthful alternatives. In fact, each of the remaining chapters of the book will show you how you can use one of the following fat substitutes:

▓ *Fruitful Fat Substitutes:* Fruit purées, applesauce, and fruit juices can replace all of the fat in cakes, muffins, quick breads, scones, and brownies, and at least half of the fat in cookies.

▓ *Dairy Fat Substitutes:* Nonfat yogurt and buttermilk can replace all of the fat in cakes, muffins, quick breads, scones, biscuits, and brownies, and at least half of the fat in cookies.

▓ *Sweet Fat Substitutes:* Liquid sweeteners like honey, molasses, jam, corn syrup, and chocolate syrup can replace all of the fat in cakes, muffins, quick breads, scones, biscuits, brownies, cookies, crumb toppings, and sweet crumb crusts.

▓ *Prunes:* Easy-to-make Prune Butter and Prune Purée can replace all of the fat in cakes, muffins, quick breads, scones, brownies, cookies, and sweet crumb crusts.

▓ *Squash and Sweet Potato:* Mashed pumpkin and other mashed squashes, as well as mashed sweet potatoes, can replace all of the fat in cakes, quick breads, muffins, biscuits, scones, and brownies, and at least half of the fat in cookies.

▓ *Reduced-Fat Margarine and Light Butter:* Contrary to popular belief, reduced-fat margarine and light butter can be used for baking, and can cut the fat in biscuits, scones, cakes, muffins, quick breads, cookies, brownies, pie crusts, and crumb toppings by more than half.

As you start reading through the recipes in this book, you'll note that some recipes use more than one kind of fat substitute. For example, a coffee cake with a crumb topping might use buttermilk to replace the fat in the batter, and a liquid sweetener to replace the fat in the crumb topping. And some of the cookie recipes use a combination of my Prune Purée and a liquid sweetener to replace the fat, as this combination produces the best texture. Realize, though, that the ingredients used as fat substitutes in this book have other functions as well. For instance, fruit purées, fruit juices, nonfat yogurt, and liquid sweeteners also serve to moisten and flavor batters. (For information about choosing and using fat substitutes in your own recipes, see the inset on page 22.)

Of course, in addition to the fat substitutes just discussed, the recipes in *Fat-Free Baking* use a number of other ingredients to create baked goods that are not only low in fat, but also nutritious and flavorful. Let's learn more about the ingredients you'll be using.

Go for the Grain

Just because a food is fat-free does not mean it is good for you. Fat-free baked goods made from refined white flour provide few nutrients, and can actually deplete nutrient stores if eaten in excess. Whole grains, on the other hand, contain a multitude of nutrients, including vitamins B-2, B-6, and E; chromium; iron; magnesium; potassium; and zinc. For this reason, many of the recipes in this book include whole wheat flour, oats, oat bran, and oat flour. These whole grain products not only add vitamins, minerals, and fiber, but also provide great taste. In fact, once accustomed to the heartier taste and texture of whole grains, most people prefer whole grains to refined flours.

Aside from the health benefits of whole grain flours, these flours offer an additional advantage. Fiber, like fat, interferes with the development of gluten, the protein in wheat flour that can cause a tough texture, tunnels, and peaked muffin tops when batters are overmixed. Since whole grain flours are rich in fiber and naturally lower in gluten than refined flours, you don't have to be too concerned about overmixing batters whenever you use these flours. However, if you decide to replace part of the whole wheat flour in these recipes with white flour, you should take special care to mix muffin and quick bread batters only until the dry ingredients become moistened.

Clearly, grains in general, and whole grains in particular, provide a wealth of benefits for both the baker and the baker's lucky family and friends. Following is a description of some of the whole grain products used throughout this book. Many of these products are readily available in grocery stores, while others may be found in health foods stores and gourmet shops. If you are unable to locate a particular flour, it is probably available by mail order. (See the Resource List on page 227.)

Barley Flour. Made from ground barley kernels, barley flour is rich in cholesterol-lowering soluble fiber. This flour is slightly sweet and adds a cake-like texture to baked goods. Barley flour can be used interchangeably with oat flour in any of the recipes in this book.

Brown Rice Flour. Made of finely ground brown rice, this flour has a texture similar to cornmeal, and adds a mildly sweet flavor to baked goods. Use it in cookies for a crisp and crunchy texture.

Cornmeal. Cornmeal adds a sweet flavor, a lovely golden color, and a crunchy texture to baked goods. For the most nutrition, be sure to buy whole grain (unbolted) cornmeal. Bolted cornmeal is nearly whole grain, while degermed cornmeal is refined.

Oat Flour. Widely available in health foods stores and many grocery stores, oat flour can also be made by grinding quick-cooking rolled oats in a blender. (Look for oats that cook in one minute.) Oat flour is rich in cholesterol-lowering soluble fiber, and has a mild, sweet flavor. This flour is a natural for fat-free baking because it retains moisture in baked goods, reducing the need for fat.

Oat Bran. Oat bran is made from the outer part of the oat kernel. It has a sweet, mild flavor, and is a concentrated source of cholesterol-lowering soluble fiber. Like oat flour, oat bran helps baked goods retain moisture. Look for oat bran in the hot cereal section of your grocery store, and choose the softer, more finely ground brands, like Quaker Oat Bran. Coarsely ground oat bran makes excellent hot cereal, but is not the best for baking.

Unbleached Flour. This is refined white flour that has not been subjected to a bleaching process. Unbleached white flour lacks significant amounts of nutrients compared with whole wheat flour, but does contain more vitamin E than bleached flour.

Wheat Bran. Unprocessed wheat bran—sometimes called miller's bran—is made from the outer portion of the whole wheat kernel. This grain product adds fiber and texture to muffins and breads.

White Whole Wheat Flour. This is an excellent option for baking. Made from hard white wheat—instead of the hard red wheat used to make regular whole wheat flour—white whole wheat flour is sweeter and lighter tasting than regular whole wheat. To substitute white whole wheat flour for other flours, use the following guidelines:

1 cup white whole wheat flour = 1 cup unbleached flour
1 cup + 1 tablespoon white whole wheat flour = 1 cup whole wheat pastry flour
1 cup + 1 tablespoon white whole wheat flour = 1 cup regular whole wheat flour

Whole Wheat Flour. This flour, made by grinding whole grain wheat kernels, includes the grain's nutrient-rich bran and germ. Nutritionally speaking, whole wheat flour is superior to refined flour. Sadly, many people grew up eating refined baked goods, and find whole grain products too heavy for their taste. A good way to learn to enjoy whole grain flours is to use part whole wheat and part unbleached flour in recipes, and gradually increase the amount of whole wheat. Use one cup plus one tablespoon unbleached flour to replace one cup of whole wheat flour.

Whole Wheat Pastry Flour. When muffin, quick bread, cake, and cookie recipes call for whole wheat flour, whole wheat pastry flour works best. Although regular whole wheat flour may be used with good results, whole wheat pastry flour produces lighter, softer-textured baked goods because it is made from a softer (low-protein) wheat and is more finely ground.

Sweeteners

Refined white sugar contains almost no nutrients. In fact, when eaten in excess, refined sugar can actually deplete body stores of essential nutrients like chromium and the B vitamins. Of course, a moderate amount of sugar is usually not a problem for people who eat an otherwise healthy diet. What's moderate? No more than 10 percent of your daily intake of calories should come from sugar. For an individual who needs 2,000 calories a day to maintain his or her weight, this amounts to an upper limit of 12.5 teaspoons (about 1/4 cup) of sugar a day. Naturally, a diet that is lower in sugar is even better.

The recipes in this book contain 25 to 50 percent less sugar than traditional recipes do. Ingredients like fruit juices, fruit purées, and dried fruits; flavorings and spices like vanilla extract, nutmeg, and cinnamon; and mildly sweet flours like oat and barley have often been used to reduce the need for sugar. As a result, the muffin and quick bread recipes average about 2 teaspoons of sugar per serving, desserts like fruit crisps contain about 3 teaspoons per serving, cakes and pies contain 3 to 6 teaspoons per serving, and cookies contain about 1 teaspoon each.

The recipes in this book call for moderate amounts of white sugar, brown sugar, and different liquid sweeteners. However, a large number of sweeteners are now available, and you should feel free to substitute one sweetener for another, using your own tastes, your desire for high-nutrient ingredients, and your pocketbook as a guide. (Some of the newer less-refined sweeteners are far more expensive than traditional sweeteners.) For best results, replace granular sweeteners with other granular sweeteners, and substitute liquid sweeteners for other liquid sweeteners. You can, of course, replace a liquid with granules, or vice versa, but adjustments in other recipe ingredients will have to be made. (For each cup of liquid sweetener substituted for granular sweetener, reduce the liquid by 1/4 to 1/3 cup.) Also be aware that each sweetener has its own unique flavor and its own degree of sweetness, making some sweeteners better suited to particular recipes. Following is a description of some of the sweeteners commonly available in grocery stores, health foods stores, and gourmet shops. Those sweeteners that can't be found in local stores can usually be ordered by mail. (See the Resource List on page 227.)

Apple Butter. Sweet and thick, apple butter is made by cooking down apples with apple juice and spices. Many brands also contain added sugar, but some are sweetened only with juice. Use apple butter as you would honey to sweeten products in which a little spice will enhance the flavor. Spice cakes, bran muffins, and oatmeal cookies are all delicious made with apple butter.

Brown Rice Syrup. Commonly available in health foods stores, brown rice syrup is made by converting the starch in brown rice into sugar. This syrup is mildly sweet—about 30 to 60 percent as sweet as sugar, depending on the brand—and has a delicate malt flavor. Perhaps most important, brown rice syrup retains most of the nutrients found in the rice from which it was made. This sweetener is a good substitute for honey or other liquid sweeteners whenever you want to tone down the sweetness of a recipe.

Brown Sugar. This granulated sweetener is simply refined white sugar that has been coated with a thin film of molasses. Light brown sugar is lighter in color than regular brown sugar, but not lower in calories as the name might imply. Because this sweetener contains some molasses, brown sugar has more calcium, iron, and potassium than white sugar. But like most sugars, brown sugar is no nutritional powerhouse. The advantage to using this sweetener is that it is more flavorful than white sugar so that less can generally be used.

Date Sugar. Made from ground dried dates, date sugar provides copper, magnesium, iron, and B vitamins. With a distinct date flavor, date sugar is delicious in breads, cakes, and muffins. Because it does not dissolve as readily as white sugar does, it's best to mix date sugar with the recipe's liquid ingredients and let it sit for a few minutes before proceeding with the recipe. Because date sugar is less dense than white sugar, it is only about two-thirds as sweet. However, date sugar is more flavorful, and so can often be substituted for white sugar on a cup-for-cup basis.

Fruit Juice Concentrates. Frozen juice concentrates add sweetness and flavor to baked goods while enhancing nutritional value. Use the concentrates as you would honey or other liquid sweeteners, but beware—too much will be overpowering. Always keep cans of frozen orange and apple juice concentrate in the freezer just for baking. Pineapple and tropical fruit blends also make good sweeteners, and white grape juice is ideal when you want a more neutral flavor.

Fruit Source. Made from white grape juice and brown rice, this sweetener has a rather neutral flavor and is about as sweet as white sugar. Fruit Source is available in both granular and liquid forms. Use the liquid as you would honey, and the granules as you would sugar. The granules do not dissolve as readily as sugar does, so mix Fruit Source with the recipe's liquid ingredients and let it sit for a few minutes before proceeding with the recipe.

Fruit Spreads, Jams, and Preserves. Available in a variety of flavors, these products make delicious sweeteners. For best flavor and nutrition, choose a brand made from fruits and fruit juice concentrate, with little or no added sugar, and select a flavor that is compatible with the baked goods you're making. Use as you would any liquid sweetener.

Honey. Contrary to popular belief, honey is not significantly more nutritious than sugar, but it does add a nice flavor to baked goods. It also adds moistness, reducing the need for fat. The sweetest of the liquid sweeteners, honey is generally 20 to 30 percent sweeter than sugar. Be sure to consider this when making substitutions.

Maple Sugar. Made from dehydrated maple syrup, maple sugar adds a distinct maple flavor to baked goods. For a change of pace, powdered maple sugar can replace powdered white sugar in glazes.

Maple Syrup. The boiled-down sap of sugar maple trees, maple syrup adds delicious flavor to all baked goods, and also provides some potassium and other nutrients. Use it as you would honey or molasses.

Molasses. Light, or Barbados, molasses is pure sugarcane juice boiled down into a thick syrup. Light molasses provides some calcium, potassium, and iron, and is delicious in spice cakes, muffins, breads, and cookies. Blackstrap molasses is a by-product of the sugar-refining process. Very rich in calcium, potassium, and iron, it has a slightly bitter, strong flavor, and is half as sweet as refined sugar. Because of its distinctive taste, more than a few tablespoons in a recipe is overwhelming.

Sucanat. Granules of evaporated sugarcane juice, Sucanat tastes similar to brown sugar. This sweetener provides small amounts of potassium, chromium, calcium, iron, and vitamins A and C. Use it as you would any other granulated sugar.

Sugarcane Syrup. The process used to make sugarcane syrup is similar to that of making light molasses. Consequently, the syrup has a molasses-like flavor and is nutritionally comparable to the other sweetener.

Throughout our discussion of sweeteners, we have mentioned that some sweeteners are higher in nutrients than others. Just how much variation is there among sweeteners? The table on page 14 compares the amounts of selected nutrients found in one-quarter cup of different sweeteners. Pay special attention to how the sweeteners compare with white sugar, the most refined of all the sweeteners.

A Word About Salt

Salt, a combination of sodium and chloride, enhances the flavors of many foods. A little salt added to a cookie, cake, or other dessert recipe can reduce the need for sugar. For this reason, some of the recipes in this book call for a small amount of salt as an optional

Sweetener (1/4 cup)	Calories	Calcium (mg)	Iron (mg)	Potassium (mg)
Apple Butter	130	10	0.5	176
Brown Rice Syrup	256	3	0.1	140
Brown Sugar	205	47	1.2	189
Date Sugar	88	10	0.4	209
Fruit Juice Concentrate (apple)	116	14	0.6	315
Fruit Juice Concentrate (orange)	113	23	0.3	479
Fruit Source (granules)	192	16	0.4	142
Fruit Source (syrup)	176	15	0.4	138
Fruit Spreads	216	8	0	12
Honey	240	0	0.5	27
Maple Sugar	176	45	0.8	137
Maple Syrup	202	83	1.0	141
Molasses, Blackstrap	170	548	20.2	2,342
Molasses, Light	172	132	4.3	732
Sucanat	144	41	1.6	162
Sugar Cane Syrup	210	48	2.9	340
White Sugar	192	1	0	2

ingredient. However, any of the recipes in this book can be made without any salt at all.

How much sodium is too much? Most health experts recommend an upper limit of 2,400 milligrams per day, the equivalent of about one teaspoonful.

Eggcetera . . .

Some of the recipes in this book call for egg whites—which are fat-free—while others call for a fat-free egg substitute. Why would one of these ingredients be listed instead of the other? Most of the time, the two ingredients can, in fact, be used interchangeably. (In recipes that require whipped egg whites, egg substitutes simply don't work. But this is the exception, rather than the rule.) However, egg substitutes are best used in some recipes simply due to ease of measuring. For example, while a recipe that calls for three tablespoons of fat-free egg substitute would work just as well with three tablespoons of egg whites, this would require you to use *one and a half* large egg whites, making measuring something of a nuisance.

If you choose to use fresh eggs but you feel wasteful throwing out all those yolks, you can substitute two large whole eggs for three egg whites in any recipe. However, keep in mind that two large eggs will add 10 grams of fat and 420 milligrams of cholesterol to the recipe. Whether substituting egg whites for egg substitute, or egg whites or egg substitute for whole eggs, use the following guidelines:

1 large egg = 1-1/2 large egg whites

1 large egg = 3 tablespoons egg substitute

1 large egg white = 2 tablespoons egg substitute

ABOUT THE NUTRITIONAL ANALYSIS

The Food Processor II (ESHA Research) computer nutritional analysis system, plus information from manufacturers, was used to calculate the nutritional information for the recipes in this book. Nutrients are always listed per one serving—one muffin, one slice of bread, one cookie, etc. When a choice of ingredients is given in a recipe, the nutritional analysis is based on the first ingredient listed.

Sometimes a recipe gives you the option of adding raisins or nuts. Should you choose to omit the nuts in your quest for fat-free eating? Keep in mind that while nuts are high in fat, they contain essential fatty acids and important minerals, as well as vitamin E. Some studies have even indicated that people who eat nuts as part of a healthy diet

TIPS FOR SUPER-MOIST FAT-FREE BAKING

The most common complaint people have about fat-free baked goods is that they are too dry. The good news is that it is possible to produce deliciously moist fat-free cakes, cookies, muffins, quick breads, and brownies. Here are some important tips that you should keep in mind as you follow the recipes in this book and create your own fat-free treats.

▨ *Avoid overbaking.* Fat-free treats bake more quickly than do those made with fat. Baked at too high a temperature or left in the oven too long, they will become dry. That's why the recipes in this book recommend lower-than-standard oven temperatures and shorter-than-standard baking times. Use the suggested baking temperatures and times as guidelines, keeping in mind that ovens do vary.

▨ *Use the toothpick test or another test of doneness.* The best way to check fat-free cakes, muffins, and quick breads for doneness is to use the toothpick test. Insert a wooden toothpick in the center of the product. As soon as the toothpick comes out clean, the product should be removed from the oven. Remove fat-free brownies from the oven as soon as the edges are firm and the center is almost set.

▨ *Adjust the amount of fat substitute.* If you follow the above guidelines for fat-free baking and your product is still dry, try adding a bit more fat substitute the next time you use that recipe. Most of the suggestions in each chapter recommend that you replace the fat in a recipe with half as much fat substitute. You should then mix up the batter and add a bit more substitute if the batter seems dry. Some recipes—especially those that are already fairly low in fat—may need a one-for-one replacement of fat substitute for fat.

> ▨ *Keep your baked goods moist and fresh.* Fat-free baked goods made with the natural fat substitutes suggested in this book will have a high moisture content and no preservatives. To keep your fat-free cookies at their freshest, place them in an airtight container and arrange them in single layers separated by sheets of waxed paper. To keep your muffins, cakes, and other baked treats moist, wrap them carefully in plastic wrap, or place them in airtight containers. Any leftovers not eaten within twenty-four hours should be refrigerated for maximum freshness. The recipes will let you know when a product must be refrigerated immediately after baking.

have a lower risk of heart disease. If you like nuts, feel free to use them in these recipes. In fat-free recipes like the ones in this book, you can afford to add a few nuts. (For more information on using nuts in your recipes, see the inset on page 184.)

Where Does the Fat Come From in Fat-Free Recipes?

You may notice that even though a recipe may contain no oil, butter, margarine, nuts, chocolate chips, or other fatty ingredients, it still contains a small amount of fat (less than one gram). This is because whole grain flours naturally contain a very small amount of oil, which is present in the germ.

The oil found in the germ of whole grains is very beneficial because it is loaded with vitamin E, as well as an abundance of other vitamins and minerals. Products made from refined grains and refined flours—ingredients that have been stripped of the germ—do have slightly less fat than whole grain versions, but also have far less nutrients.

Looking at Labels

A variety of fat-free baked goods are available in grocery stores. The nutrition information label usually shows the product to contain zero grams of fat. Be aware, though, that a product can list its fat grams as zero and claim to be fat-free if it contains less than 0.5 grams of fat per serving. In other words, even if a product actually contains 0.4 grams of fat per serving, the product label can list the fat grams as zero.

The Nutritional Facts analyses that follow each of the recipes in this book list *actual* amounts of fat rather than rounding down to zero. With the exception of the recipes in Chapter 7, none of the recipes in this book contains any added fats or oils.

Eat Well and Enjoy!

Making the change to a low-fat lifestyle should not mean dieting and deprivation. This book is filled with recipes for moist, delicious, and satisfying baked treats that maximize nutrition not only by eliminating or reducing fat, but also by using whole grain flours, unrefined sweeteners, and other healthful ingredients whenever possible. The muffins, breads, cakes, and other baked goods that you're about to make are not just delicious. They are foods that you can feel good about serving to your family and friends.

Probably the best feature of this book, though, is that it will enable you to enjoy your own favorite recipes—minus the fat. By following the simple guidelines provided at the beginning of each chapter, you'll be able to successfully replace the fat in most of your homemade baked goods. If you are new to low-fat eating, it is a good idea to start by replacing only half the fat at first. Evaluate the results, and try using even less fat next time. Soon you will have a new and improved fat-free family favorite.

FRUITFUL FAT SUBSTITUTES

ruit purées and juices make excellent fat sub-stitutes in cakes, breads, cookies, muffins, and many other baked goods. Besides eliminating fat and excess calories, these tasty ingredients add fla-vor and sweetness, reducing the need for sugar.

Through years of experimentation, I have found that different purées and juices work best in different recipes. For instance, apple-sauce is an especially good fat substitute in gingerbread, chocolate cakes, white cakes, and recipes in which you do not want to change the original flavor. Apple butter is an excellent fat substitute in spice cakes and bran muffins. Mashed bananas are delicious in muffins, quick breads, and chocolate cakes. Or you might try apple and orange juice in carrot cakes, puréed pears in quick breads and coffee cakes, and puréed peaches in muffins and spice cakes.

GETTING THE FAT OUT

Below, you'll find some basic guidelines that will help you successfully replace the fat in your own recipes. (For more helpful hints on modifying recipes, see the inset on page 22.) After these guidelines, you'll find tried-and-true recipes for muffins, breads, cakes, and other sweet treats that have been made more healthy and delicious with the addition of fruitful fat substitutes.

CAKE, MUFFIN, AND QUICK BREAD RECIPES

▓ Replace all or part of the butter, margarine, or other solid shortening in cake, muffin, and quick bread recipes with half as much applesauce, apple butter, fruit juice, or puréed fruit. If the recipe calls for oil, replace all or part of the oil with three-fourths as much fat substitute. Mix up the batter. If it seems too dry, add a little more fat substitute. Some recipes may need a one-for-one substitution.

▓ When eliminating all of the fat from a recipe, reduce the number of eggs by half, or substitute 1 egg white for each whole egg. This will help preserve tenderness. In some recipes, you may be able to eliminate the eggs altogether by replacing each whole egg with 2 tablespoons of fat substitute or another liquid. Fat-free quick breads and chocolate cakes, for instance, do well without eggs.

▓ To retain moistness, bake fat-free and fat-reduced cakes, muffins, and quick breads at a slightly lower-than-standard temperature. Bake muffins at 350°F. Bake quick breads and cakes at 325°F to 350°F. *Be careful not to overbake.* Bake just until a wooden toothpick inserted in the center comes out clean.

BISCUIT AND SCONE RECIPES

▓ Replace all or part of the butter, margarine, or other solid shortening in biscuit and scone recipes with half as much applesauce or fruit purée. (Juices do not work well in these recipes.) If the recipe calls for oil, replace all or part of the oil with three-fourths as much applesauce or fruit purée. Mix up the dough. If it seems too stiff, add more fat substitute.

- When eliminating all of the fat from a biscuit or scone recipe, reduce the number of eggs by half, or substitute 1 egg white for each whole egg.
- Bake fat-free biscuits and scones at 375°F.

BROWNIE RECIPES

- Replace all of the butter, margarine, or other solid shortening in brownie recipes with half as much applesauce or fruit purée. If the recipe calls for oil, replace all of the oil with three-fourths as much fat substitute. Mix up the batter. If it seems too dry, add a bit more substitute. In some recipes—especially those made with oil—you will have to replace the fat with an equal amount of the fruit.
- When eliminating all of the fat from a brownie recipe, you may replace each whole egg with 3 tablespoons of fat-free egg substitute if desired. However, it is not necessary to reduce the number of eggs.
- Bake fat-free brownies at 325°F, and check for doneness a few minutes before the end of the usual baking time. Remove the brownies from the oven as soon as the edges are firm and the center is almost set.

COOKIE RECIPES

- Replace half of the butter, margarine, or other solid shortening in cookie recipes with half as much applesauce, mashed banana, or fruit purée. For example, if the recipe calls for 1 cup of butter, use 1/2 cup of butter and 1/4 cup of your chosen fat substitute. If the recipe calls for oil, replace half of the oil with three-fourths as much fat substitute. (You can replace more than half the fat, but the cookies may take on a cakey or rubbery texture. Cookies that contain a high proportion of oats or oat bran are the easiest to make fat-free.)
- When reducing the fat in a cookie recipe, you may replace each whole egg with 3 tablespoons of fat-free egg substitute if desired. However, it is not necessary to reduce the number of eggs.
- Bake reduced-fat cookies at 275°F to 300°F.

CHOOSING AND USING FAT SUBSTITUTES IN YOUR OWN RECIPES

As you create fat-free versions of your own favorite recipes, use the following guidelines as a starting point. Once you've chosen the fat substitute that you want to use—fruit juice, for instance—you can then turn to the chapter that focuses on that substitute for more specific tips.

▓ Choose a fat substitute that is compatible with your recipe. How? Start by taking a look at the ingredients in your recipe. Very likely, the recipe already contains a logical fat substitute, such as applesauce, fruit purée, fruit juice, buttermilk, or yogurt. If so, this ingredient will be your best choice, and you need only increase the amount of this product as you eliminate the fat. The chapter dealing with that substitute will give you a specific formula for doing so.

If your recipe does *not* contain a logical fat substitute, consider the flavors that would best blend with that recipe. For instance, substitutes such as applesauce, mashed banana, mashed cooked pumpkin, maple syrup, and prunes would all be delicious in a spice cake. On the other hand, when making biscuits and other baked goods with fairly subtle flavors, you will probably want to choose a mild-tasting fat substitute like nonfat buttermilk or plain nonfat yogurt.

▓ Realize that some recipes are better candidates for fat-reduction than others. Quick breads and muffins are some of the most easily adapted recipes. Coffee cakes, chocolate cakes, carrot cakes, spice cakes, and other cakes that naturally have denser textures also are easily made fat-free. Cakes that are meant to have a very light, tender texture are the most difficult to modify. However, you can easily eliminate one-half to three-fourths of the fat even in these recipes.

In most cookie recipes, fat substitutes like fruit purées, nonfat buttermilk, nonfat yogurt, and mashed cooked pumpkin can easily replace half the fat, while liquid sweeteners, prune purée, and prune butter can replace all of the fat. However, keep in mind that cookie recipes are easiest to adapt when they do not already contain significant amounts of liquid ingredients like applesauce, mashed banana, or buttermilk. Too much liquid can give cookies a cakey or rubbery texture.

▓ Cakes made with butter, margarine, or another solid shortening get some of their volume from the air that is incorporated into the batter when the fat is creamed with the sugar. When you eliminate all of the fat from these cakes, they become more compact. To offset this, try whipping the egg whites and gently folding them into the cake batter.

▓ Realize that when you replace solid fats like butter and margarine with a fat substitute, you must change the way the recipe's ingredients are mixed. Instead of creaming the substitute with the sugar, add the substitute along with the recipe's liquid ingredients.

▓ Start by replacing only half the fat in your recipe. Evaluate the results, and, if desired, reduce the fat even more the next time you use that recipe.

▓ When eliminating all of the fat in a recipe, it is a good idea to substitute a whole grain flour for at least one-third to one-half of the refined flour used in the recipe. Oats, oat bran, and wheat bran may also be used to replace part of the flour. The fiber in these ingredients will help maintain a pleasing texture in your baked goods.

▓ If you have replaced all of the fat according to the chapter guidelines and your product has a slightly tough, coarse texture, try adding a tablespoon or two of lecithin granules to the recipe. Lecithin, a by-product of soy oil refining, greatly improves the texture of baked goods. In fact, it is a common ingredient in many commercial fat-free cakes. Lecithin is readily available in health foods stores. (For more information on lecithin, see the inset on page 83.)

After making several of the recipes found in this book, you'll begin to get a "feel" for fat-free baking. This experience—along with the guidelines presented in this book and some trial and error—is sure to help you successfully reduce or eliminate the fat in all your homemade treats.

APPLESAUCE MAPLE MUFFINS

Yield: 12 muffins

NUTRITIONAL FACTS
(PER MUFFIN)

CALORIES: 130

FAT: 0.4 G

PROTEIN: 3.6 G

CHOLESTEROL: 0 MG

SODIUM: 94 MG

FIBER: 3.3 G

CALCIUM: 26 MG

POTASSIUM: 188 MG

IRON: 1 MG

2 cups whole wheat flour

1 tablespoon baking powder

1-1/4 cups unsweetened applesauce

1/2 cup maple syrup

2 egg whites

1/2 cup dark raisins or chopped walnuts

1. Combine the flour and baking powder, and stir to mix well. Add the applesauce, maple syrup, and egg whites, and stir just until the dry ingredients are moistened. Fold in the raisins or walnuts.

2. Coat muffin cups with nonstick cooking spray, and fill 3/4 full with the batter. Bake at 350°F for 16 to 18 minutes, or just until a wooden toothpick inserted in the center of a muffin comes out clean.

3. Remove the muffin tin from the oven, and allow it to sit for 5 minutes before removing the muffins. Serve warm or at room temperature.

ORANGE OATMEAL MUFFINS

Yield: 12 muffins

NUTRITIONAL FACTS
(PER MUFFIN)

CALORIES: 131	
FAT: 0.7 G	
PROTEIN: 4.1 G	
CHOLESTEROL: 0 MG	
SODIUM: 106 MG	
FIBER: 2.8 G	
CALCIUM: 17 MG	
POTASSIUM: 150 MG	
IRON: 1 MG	

1 cup quick-cooking oats

1 cup plus 2 tablespoons orange juice

1-1/2 cups whole wheat flour

1/2 cup sugar

1 teaspoon baking powder

1 teaspoon baking soda

2 egg whites

Topping:

3 tablespoons quick-cooking oats

1 tablespoon frozen orange juice
concentrate, thawed

1-1/2 teaspoons sugar

1. To make the topping, combine the topping ingredients until crumbly. Set aside.

2. Combine the oats and orange juice, and set aside for 20 minutes.

3. Combine the flour, sugar, baking powder, and baking soda, and stir to mix well. Add the orange juice mixture and the egg whites to the flour mixture, and stir just until the dry ingredients are moistened.

4. Coat muffin cups with nonstick cooking spray, and fill 3/4 full with the batter. Sprinkle the topping over the batter. Bake at 350°F for 14 to 16 minutes, or just until a wooden toothpick inserted in the center of a muffin comes out clean.

5. Remove the muffin tin from the oven, and allow it to sit for 5 minutes before removing the muffins. Serve warm or at room temperature.

VERY CRANBERRY MUFFINS

Yield: 12 muffins

NUTRITIONAL FACTS
(PER MUFFIN)

CALORIES: 137	
FAT: 0.7 G	
PROTEIN: 4.2 G	
CHOLESTEROL: 0 MG	
SODIUM: 107 MG	
FIBER: 3.1 G	
CALCIUM: 44 MG	
POTASSIUM: 125 MG	
IRON: 0.9 MG	

1 cup quick-cooking oats

3/4 cup skim milk

1-1/2 cups whole wheat flour

1 tablespoon baking powder

1/4 cup sugar

1 cup whole berry cranberry sauce

2 egg whites

1 teaspoon vanilla extract

1/4 cup chopped walnuts (optional)

1   Combine the oats and milk, and set aside for 15 minutes.

2   Combine the flour, baking powder, and sugar, and stir to mix well. Add the oat mixture and the remaining ingredients, and stir just until the dry ingredients are moistened.

3   Coat muffin cups with nonstick cooking spray, and fill 3/4 full with the batter. Bake at 350°F for about 18 minutes, or just until a wooden toothpick inserted in the center of a muffin comes out clean.

4   Remove the muffin tin from the oven, and allow it to sit for 5 minutes before removing the muffins. Serve warm or at room temperature.

MANDARIN BLUEBERRY MUFFINS

Yield: 12 muffins

NUTRITIONAL FACTS (PER MUFFIN)
CALORIES: 113
FAT: 0.7 G
PROTEIN: 4.2 G
CHOLESTEROL: 0 MG
SODIUM: 94 MG
FIBER: 3.9 G
CALCIUM: 28 MG
POTASSIUM: 155 MG
IRON: 1.1 MG

1-3/4 cups whole wheat flour

3/4 cup oat bran

1/3 cup sugar

1 tablespoon baking powder

1 can (11 ounces) mandarin orange segments in light syrup, undrained

2 egg whites

1 teaspoon vanilla or almond extract

1/2 cup plus 2 tablespoons fresh or frozen blueberries

1 Combine the flour, oat bran, sugar, and baking powder, and stir to mix well. Crush the orange segments slightly and add the oranges and their syrup, the egg whites, and the vanilla extract to the flour mixture, and stir just until the dry ingredients are moistened. Fold in the blueberries.

2 Coat muffin cups with nonstick cooking spray, and fill 3/4 full with the batter. Bake at 350°F for 15 to 18 minutes, or just until a wooden toothpick inserted in the center of a muffin comes out clean.

3 Remove the muffin tin from the oven, and allow it to sit for 5 minutes before removing the muffins. Serve warm or at room temperature.

BROWN SUGAR BANANA MUFFINS

Yield: 12 muffins

NUTRITIONAL FACTS
(PER MUFFIN)

CALORIES: 121

FAT: 0.5 G

PROTEIN: 3.7 G

CHOLESTEROL: 0 MG

SODIUM: 97 MG

FIBER: 3.1 G

CALCIUM: 31 MG

POTASSIUM: 234 MG

IRON: 1.1 MG

2 cups whole wheat flour

1/3 cup brown sugar

1 tablespoon baking powder

1 cup mashed very ripe banana
    (about 2 large)

1/3 cup skim milk

1 teaspoon vanilla extract

2 egg whites

Topping:

1 tablespoon brown sugar

1 tablespoon toasted wheat germ

1 To make the topping, stir together the brown sugar and wheat germ, and set aside.

2 Combine the flour, brown sugar, and baking powder, and stir to mix well. Add the banana, skim milk, vanilla extract, and egg whites, and stir just until the dry ingredients are moistened.

3 Coat muffin cups with nonstick cooking spray, and fill 3/4 full with the batter. Sprinkle the topping over the batter. Bake at 350°F for 14 to 16 minutes, or just until a wooden toothpick inserted in the center of a muffin comes out clean.

4 Remove the muffin tin from the oven, and allow it to sit for 5 minutes before removing the muffins. Serve warm or at room temperature.

PEACHY BRAN MUFFINS

Yield: 12 muffins

NUTRITIONAL FACTS (PER MUFFIN)
CALORIES: 121
FAT: 0.5 G
PROTEIN: 3.5 G
CHOLESTEROL: 0 MG
SODIUM: 94 MG
FIBER: 3.3 G
CALCIUM: 26 MG
POTASSIUM: 183 MG
IRON: 1.1 MG

1-1/2 cups whole wheat flour

2/3 cup wheat bran

1/2 cup sugar

1 tablespoon baking powder

1 can (1 pound) peaches packed in juice, undrained

2 egg whites

1/3 cup chopped dried peaches or chopped pecans

1 Combine the flour, wheat bran, sugar, and baking powder, and stir to mix well. Set aside.

2 Drain the peaches, reserving the juice, and purée in a blender. Add enough juice to the puréed peaches to bring the volume up to 1-1/2 cups. Add the peach purée and the egg whites to the flour mixture, and stir just until the dry ingredients are moistened. Fold in the dried peaches or pecans.

3 Coat muffin cups with nonstick cooking spray, and fill 3/4 full with the batter. Bake at 350°F for 15 to 17 minutes, or just until a wooden toothpick inserted in the center of a muffin comes out clean.

4 Remove the muffin tin from the oven, and allow it to sit for 5 minutes before removing the muffins. Serve warm or at room temperature.

THREE-GRAIN MUFFINS

Yield: 12 muffins

NUTRITIONAL FACTS
(PER MUFFIN)

CALORIES: 110

FAT: 0.9 G

PROTEIN: 4.1 G

CHOLESTEROL: 0 MG

SODIUM: 135 MG

FIBER: 4 G

CALCIUM: 42 MG

POTASSIUM: 267 MG

IRON: 1.7 MG

1-1/2 cups wheat bran

3/4 cup plus 2 tablespoons oat bran

1/2 cup whole grain cornmeal

1/3 cup brown sugar

1-1/2 teaspoons baking soda

3/4 cup apple or prune juice

1 cup nonfat buttermilk

3 tablespoons fat-free egg substitute

1 teaspoon vanilla extract

1/2 cup dark raisins or chopped dried apricots

1 Combine the wheat bran, oat bran, cornmeal, brown sugar, and baking soda, and stir to mix well. Add the remaining ingredients, and stir just until the dry ingredients are moistened. Cover, and refrigerate at least overnight. (This batter may be refrigerated for up to a week.)

2 Coat muffin cups with nonstick cooking spray, and fill 3/4 full with the batter. Bake at 350°F for about 18 minutes, or until a wooden toothpick inserted in the center of a muffin comes out clean.

3 Remove the muffin tin from the oven, and allow it to sit for 5 minutes before removing the muffins. Serve warm or at room temperature.

CHOCOLATE CRUMB MUFFINS

Yield: 12 muffins

NUTRITIONAL FACTS
(PER MUFFIN)

CALORIES: 147	
FAT: 1.4 G	
PROTEIN: 4 G	
CHOLESTEROL: 0 MG	
SODIUM: 119 MG	
FIBER: 3.8 G	
CALCIUM: 39 MG	
POTASSIUM: 174 MG	
IRON: 1.6 MG	

1 cup whole wheat flour

1 cup oat flour

1/4 cup plus 2 tablespoons cocoa powder

1/2 cup light brown sugar

1 tablespoon baking powder

1 can (1 pound) pear halves packed in juice, undrained

2 egg whites

1 teaspoon vanilla extract

Topping:

1/4 cup plus 2 tablespoons quick-cooking oats

1 tablespoon cocoa powder

1 tablespoon brown sugar

1 tablespoon honey

1 To make the topping, combine the oats, cocoa, and brown sugar, and stir to mix well. Add the honey and stir until the mixture is moist and crumbly. Set aside.

2 Combine the flours, cocoa, brown sugar, and baking powder, and stir to mix well. Place the pears and their juice in a blender, and purée until smooth. Add 1-1/2 cups of this mixture to the flour mixture. (Reserve the remaining purée for use in another recipe.) Add the egg whites and vanilla extract, and stir just until the dry ingredients are moistened.

3 Coat muffin cups with nonstick cooking spray, and fill 3/4 full with the batter. Sprinkle a rounded teaspoonful of the topping over each muffin, and press very lightly into the batter. Bake at 350°F for 14 to

16 minutes, or just until a wooden toothpick inserted in the center of a muffin comes out clean.

4 Remove the muffin tin from the oven, and allow it to sit for 5 minutes before removing the muffins. Serve warm or at room temperature.

ORANGE POPPY SEED BREAD

Yield: 16 slices

NUTRITIONAL FACTS (PER SLICE)
CALORIES: 84
FAT: 0.5 G
PROTEIN: 2.2 G
CHOLESTEROL: 0 MG
SODIUM: 52 MG
FIBER: 2 G
CALCIUM: 14 MG
POTASSIUM: 91 MG
IRON: 0.7 MG

2 cups whole wheat flour
1/2 cup sugar
1 teaspoon baking soda
1 tablespoon poppy seeds
1 cup orange juice
1 teaspoon vanilla extract

1 Combine the flour, sugar, baking soda, and poppy seeds, and stir to mix well. Add the orange juice and vanilla extract, and stir just until the dry ingredients are moistened.

2 Coat an 8-x-4-inch loaf pan with nonstick cooking spray. Spread the mixture evenly in the pan, and bake at 325°F for about 45 minutes, or just until a wooden toothpick inserted in the center of the loaf comes out clean.

3 Remove bread from oven, and let sit for 10 minutes. Invert loaf onto a wire rack, turn right side up, and cool before slicing and serving.

PUMPKIN SPICE BREAD

Yield: 16 slices

NUTRITIONAL FACTS (PER SLICE)	
CALORIES:	82
FAT:	0.4 G
PROTEIN:	1.5 G
CHOLESTEROL:	0 MG
SODIUM:	74 MG
FIBER:	2 G
CALCIUM:	13 MG
POTASSIUM:	93 MG
IRON:	0.8 MG

1-3/4 cups whole wheat flour
1/2 cup sugar
1-1/2 teaspoons pumpkin pie spice
1 teaspoon baking soda
1 teaspoon baking powder
1 cup cooked mashed pumpkin
1/2 cup apple or orange juice
1/4 cup chopped pecans (optional)

1. Combine the flour, sugar, pumpkin pie spice, baking soda, and baking powder, and stir to mix well. Add the pumpkin and apple or orange juice, and stir just until the dry ingredients are moistened. Fold in the nuts if desired.

2. Coat an 8-x-4-inch loaf pan with nonstick cooking spray. Spread the mixture evenly in the pan, and bake at 350°F for 40 to 45 minutes, or just until a wooden toothpick inserted in the center of the loaf comes out clean.

3. Remove the bread from the oven, and let sit for 10 minutes. Invert the loaf onto a wire rack, turn right side up, and cool before slicing and serving.

SUPER-MOIST APPLE BREAD

Yield: 16 slices

NUTRITIONAL FACTS
(PER SLICE)

CALORIES: 89

FAT: 0.3 G

PROTEIN: 2 G

CHOLESTEROL: 0 MG

SODIUM: 54 MG

FIBER: 2.2 G

CALCIUM: 13 MG

POTASSIUM: 114 MG

IRON: 0.8 MG

2 cups whole wheat flour

1/2 cup brown sugar

1 teaspoon baking soda

3/4 cup apple juice

1 teaspoon vanilla extract

2 cups finely chopped apples

1/4 cup chopped dark raisins or chopped walnuts (optional)

1 Combine the flour, brown sugar, and baking soda, and stir to mix well. Add the apple juice and vanilla extract, and stir just until the dry ingredients are moistened. Fold in the apples. Fold in the raisins or walnuts if desired.

2 Coat an 8-x-4-inch loaf pan with nonstick cooking spray. Spread the mixture evenly in the pan, and bake at 325°F for 50 to 55 minutes, or just until a wooden toothpick inserted in the center of the loaf comes out clean.

3 Remove the bread from the oven, and let sit for 10 minutes. Invert the loaf onto a wire rack, turn right side up, and cool before slicing and serving.

FRUITFUL CRANBERRY BREAD

Yield: 16 slices

NUTRITIONAL FACTS (PER SLICE)
CALORIES: 76
FAT: 0.5 G
PROTEIN: 2.2 G
CHOLESTEROL: 0 MG
SODIUM: 73 MG
FIBER: 2.5 G
CALCIUM: 12 MG
POTASSIUM: 126 MG
IRON: 0.7 MG

1-1/2 cups whole wheat flour

1/2 cup oat bran

1/3 cup sugar

1 teaspoon baking powder

1 teaspoon baking soda

3/4 cup orange or apple juice

1/2 cup mashed very ripe banana (about 1 large)

1 teaspoon vanilla extract

1 cup coarsely chopped fresh or frozen cranberries

1 Combine the flour, oat bran, sugar, baking powder, and baking soda, and stir to mix well. Add the juice, banana, and vanilla extract, and stir just until the dry ingredients are moistened. Fold in the cranberries.

2 Coat an 8-x-4-inch loaf pan with nonstick cooking spray. Spread the mixture evenly in the pan, and bake at 350°F for about 45 minutes, or just until a wooden toothpick inserted in the center of the loaf comes out clean.

3 Remove the bread from the oven, and let sit for 10 minutes. Invert the loaf onto a wire rack, turn right side up, and cool before slicing and serving.

HONEY BANANA BREAD

Yield: 16 slices

2 cups whole wheat flour

1/4 cup brown sugar

1-1/2 teaspoons baking powder

3/4 teaspoon baking soda

1/4 teaspoon ground nutmeg

1 cup mashed very ripe banana (about 2 large)

1/3 cup honey

1/4 cup skim milk

1. Combine the flour, brown sugar, baking powder, baking soda, and nutmeg, and stir to mix well. Add the banana, honey, and milk, and stir just until the dry ingredients are moistened.

2. Coat an 8-x-4-inch loaf pan with nonstick cooking spray. Spread the mixture evenly in the pan, and bake at 325°F for 45 to 50 minutes, or just until a wooden toothpick inserted in the center of the loaf comes out clean.

3. Remove the bread from the oven, and let sit for 10 minutes. Invert the loaf onto a wire rack, turn right side up, and cool before slicing and serving.

CARROT FRUIT BREAD

Yield: 16 slices

1-1/2 cups whole wheat flour

1 teaspoon baking powder

1 teaspoon baking soda

1/2 cup brown sugar

1/4 cup plus 1 tablespoon orange or pineapple juice

2 egg whites

1 teaspoon almond extract

1-1/4 cups grated carrots

1/3 cup chopped dates

1/3 cup chopped dried apricots

1 Combine the flour, baking powder, baking soda, and brown sugar, and stir to mix well. Add the juice, egg whites, and almond extract, and stir just until the dry ingredients are moistened. Fold in the remaining ingredients.

2 Coat an 8-x-4-inch loaf pan with nonstick cooking spray. Spread the mixture evenly in the pan, and bake at 350°F for about 45 minutes, or just until a wooden toothpick inserted in the center of the loaf comes out clean.

3 Remove the bread from the oven, and let sit for 10 minutes. Invert the loaf onto a wire rack, turn right side up, and cool before slicing and serving.

FABULOUS FRUITCAKE

Yield: 20 slices

NUTRITIONAL FACTS
(PER SLICE)
CALORIES: 101
FAT: 0.2 G
PROTEIN: 2 G
CHOLESTEROL: 0 MG
SODIUM: 17 MG
FIBER: 2.9 G
CALCIUM: 18 MG
POTASSIUM: 306 MG
IRON: 1.2 MG

1 cup whole wheat flour
1/4 cup light brown sugar
1/2 teaspoon baking powder
3/4 cup unsweetened applesauce
2 egg whites
2/3 cup whole dried apricots
2/3 cup dried pineapple chunks
2/3 cup whole pitted prunes
1/2 cup golden raisins
1/2 cup chopped dried dates or chopped walnuts

1 Combine the flour, brown sugar, and baking powder, and stir to mix well. Add the applesauce and egg whites, and stir to mix well. Fold in the fruits.

2 Coat two 5-x-3-inch loaf pans with nonstick cooking spray. Divide the mixture evenly between the pans and bake at 325°F for about 45 minutes, or just until a wooden toothpick inserted in the center of each loaf comes out clean.

3 Remove the bread from the oven, and let sit for 10 minutes. Invert the loaves onto a wire rack, turn right side up, and cool to room temperature. Wrap the bread in foil and let sit overnight before slicing and serving.

CHERRY APPLE SCONES

Yield: 12 scones

NUTRITIONAL FACTS (PER SCONE)
CALORIES: 118
FAT: 0.3 G
PROTEIN: 3.1 G
CHOLESTEROL: 0 MG
SODIUM: 95 MG
FIBER: 1.8 G
CALCIUM: 18 MG
POTASSIUM: 99 MG
IRON: 1.1 MG

If you are unable to find dried cherries, substitute golden raisins or dried cranberries.

1-1/2 cups unbleached flour

3/4 cup whole wheat flour

3 tablespoons sugar

2 teaspoons baking powder

1/2 teaspoon baking soda

1 egg white

3/4 cup plus 2 tablespoons unsweetened applesauce

1/3 cup dried cherries

Skim milk or 1 beaten egg white

1 Combine the flours, sugar, baking powder, and baking soda, and stir to mix well. Stir in the egg white and just enough of the applesauce to form a stiff dough. Stir in the dried cherries.

2 Form the dough into a ball, and turn onto a lightly floured surface. With floured hands, pat the dough into a 7-inch circle.

3 Coat a baking sheet with nonstick cooking spray. Place the dough on the sheet, and use a sharp floured knife to cut it into 12 wedges. Pull the wedges out slightly to leave a 1/2-inch space between them. Brush the tops lightly with skim milk or beaten egg white.

4 Bake at 375°F for about 20 minutes, or until lightly browned. Transfer to a serving plate, and serve hot with cherry fruit spread or apple jelly.

Top: Orange Poppy Seed Bread (page 33)
Bottom Left: Pumpkin Spice Bread (page 34)
Bottom Right: Carrot Fruit Bread (page 38)

Top: Cocoa Streusel Cake (page 56)
Bottom: Apple Butter Bundt Cake (page 46)

Top Left: **Oatmeal Fudge Squares (page 57)**
Top Right: **West Indian Bread Pudding (page 61)**
Bottom: **Fat-Free Fudge Brownies (page 58)**

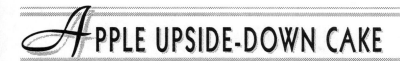

APPLE UPSIDE-DOWN CAKE

Yield: 10 servings

NUTRITIONAL FACTS
(PER SERVING)

CALORIES: 179

FAT: 0.4 G

PROTEIN: 2.7 G

CHOLESTEROL: 0 MG

SODIUM: 94 MG

FIBER: 1.6 G

CALCIUM: 12 MG

POTASSIUM: 138 MG

IRON: 1.2 MG

2 tablespoons frozen apple juice
  concentrate, thawed

1/4 cup brown sugar

2 medium apples, peeled and sliced
  1/4 inch thick

1 cup unbleached flour

1/2 cup whole wheat flour

3/4 cup sugar

1 teaspoon baking soda

1/8 teaspoon ground nutmeg

1 cup apple juice

3 tablespoons fat-free egg substitute

1 Coat a 9-inch ovenproof skillet with nonstick cooking spray. Spread the apple juice concentrate over the bottom of the skillet, and sprinkle with the brown sugar. Arrange the apple slices in a circular pattern over the brown sugar. Set aside.

2 Combine the flours, sugar, baking soda, and nutmeg, and stir to mix well. Stir in the apple juice and egg substitute. Pour the batter over the apples, and bake at 350°F for 25 to 30 minutes, or just until a wooden toothpick inserted in the center of the cake comes out clean.

3 Cool at room temperature for 25 minutes; then invert onto a serving platter. Cut into wedges and serve warm or at room temperature.

FRESH APPLE CAKE

Yield: 16 servings

NUTRITIONAL FACTS *(PER SERVING)*
CALORIES: 163
FAT: 0.3 G
PROTEIN: 2.6 G
CHOLESTEROL: 0 MG
SODIUM: 78 MG
FIBER: 1 G
CALCIUM: 7 MG
POTASSIUM: 69 MG
IRON: 1 MG

1-1/2 cups unbleached flour

1 cup whole wheat flour

1-1/2 cups sugar

1-1/4 teaspoons baking soda

1-1/4 teaspoons ground cinnamon

3/4 cup apple juice

3 egg whites

2 teaspoons vanilla extract

3 cups thinly sliced fresh apples
 (about 3-1/2 medium)

1/2 cup chopped walnuts (optional)

1 Combine the flours, sugar, baking soda, and cinnamon, and stir to mix well. Add the apple juice, egg whites, and vanilla extract, and stir to mix well. Fold in the apples and walnuts.

2 Coat a 9-x-13-inch pan with nonstick cooking spray. Spread the batter evenly in the pan, and bake at 325°F for 40 to 50 minutes, or just until a wooden toothpick inserted in the center of the cake comes out clean.

3 Cool the cake for at least 20 minutes. Cut into squares and serve warm or at room temperature with a light whipped topping if desired.

APPLESAUCE GINGERBREAD

Yield: 16 servings

NUTRITIONAL FACTS
(PER SERVING)

CALORIES: 157

FAT: 0.3 G

PROTEIN: 3.1 G

CHOLESTEROL: 0 MG

SODIUM: 146 MG

FIBER: 1.6 G

CALCIUM: 38 MG

POTASSIUM: 255 MG

IRON: 1.7 MG

1-1/2 cups unbleached flour

1 cup whole wheat flour

2/3 cup sugar

2-1/2 teaspoons baking soda

1 teaspoon ground ginger

1 teaspoon ground cinnamon

1 teaspoon ground allspice

1-1/2 cups unsweetened applesauce

1 cup molasses

3 egg whites

1 Combine the flours, sugar, baking soda, and spices, and stir to mix well. Add the remaining ingredients, and stir to mix well.

2 Coat a 9-x-13-inch pan with nonstick cooking spray. Spread the batter evenly in the pan, and bake at 325°F for 40 minutes, or just until a wooden toothpick inserted in the center of the cake comes out clean.

3 Cool the cake for at least 20 minutes. Cut into squares and serve warm or at room temperature with a light whipped topping if desired.

APPLE SPICE COFFEE CAKE

Yield: 8 servings

NUTRITIONAL FACTS
(PER SERVING)

CALORIES: 185	
FAT: 0.9 G	
PROTEIN: 4.0 G	
CHOLESTEROL: 0 MG	
SODIUM: 136 MG	
FIBER: 1.8 G	
CALCIUM: 45 MG	
POTASSIUM: 187 MG	
IRON: 1.7 MG	

1/2 cup whole wheat flour

1 cup unbleached flour

1/2 cup brown sugar

1 teaspoon baking soda

1/4 teaspoon ground cloves

1/2 teaspoon ground cinnamon

1/3 cup apple butter

2/3 cup nonfat buttermilk

1 egg white

3/4 cup finely chopped fresh apples
   (about 1 medium)

Topping:

1 tablespoon finely ground walnuts

1 tablespoon brown sugar

1 To make the topping, stir together the walnuts and brown sugar. Set aside.

2 Combine the flours, brown sugar, baking soda, and spices, and stir to mix well. Stir in the apple butter, buttermilk, and egg white. Fold in the chopped apple.

3 Coat an 8-inch round cake pan with nonstick cooking spray. Spread the batter evenly in the pan, and sprinkle with the topping. Bake at 325°F for 30 to 35 minutes, or just until a wooden toothpick inserted in the center of the cake comes out clean.

4 Cool the cake for at least 20 minutes. Cut into wedges and serve warm or at room temperature.

BROWN SUGAR AND SPICE CAKE

Yield: 16 servings

NUTRITIONAL FACTS
(PER SERVING)

CALORIES: 197

FAT: 0.6 G

PROTEIN: 7.3 G

CHOLESTEROL: 0 MG

SODIUM: 164 MG

FIBER: 1.5 G

CALCIUM: 188 MG

POTASSIUM: 176 MG

IRON: 1.5 MG

The spice in this cake is supplied by the apple butter.

1 cup whole wheat flour

1-2/3 cups unbleached flour

1 cup light brown sugar

1 teaspoon baking powder

1-1/2 teaspoons baking soda

1-1/3 cups nonfat buttermilk

3/4 cup apple butter

2 egg whites

Icing:

15 ounces nonfat ricotta cheese

1/4 cup confectioners' sugar

1 teaspoon vanilla or maple extract

1/4 cup apple butter

1 Combine the flours, brown sugar, baking powder, and baking soda, and stir to mix well. Stir in the buttermilk, apple butter, and egg whites.

2 Coat a 9-x-13-inch pan with nonstick cooking spray. Spread the batter evenly in the pan, and bake at 325°F for about 35 minutes, or just until a wooden toothpick inserted in the center of the cake comes out clean. Cool the cake to room temperature.

3 To make the icing, place the ricotta cheese in a food processor, and process until smooth. Add the confectioners' sugar and vanilla or maple extract, and process to mix well. Add the apple butter, and process just long enough to mix well.

4 Spread the icing over the cooled cake. Cut into squares and serve immediately or refrigerate.

APPLE BUTTER BUNDT CAKE

Yield: 16 servings

NUTRITIONAL FACTS
(PER SERVING)
CALORIES: 146
FAT: 0.6 G
PROTEIN: 2.9 G
CHOLESTEROL: 0 MG
SODIUM: 111 MG
FIBER: 2 G
CALCIUM: 12 MG
POTASSIUM: 185 MG
IRON: 1.1 MG

3/4 cup whole wheat flour

1-1/2 cups unbleached flour

2 teaspoons baking soda

2 cups apple butter

2 egg whites

1/2 cup dark raisins

1-1/2 tablespoons confectioners' sugar

1 Combine the flours and baking soda, and stir to mix well. Add the apple butter and egg whites, and stir to mix well. Stir in the raisins.

2 Coat a 12-cup bundt pan with nonstick cooking spray. Spread the batter evenly in the pan, and bake at 350°F for 30 to 35 minutes, or just until a wooden toothpick inserted in the center of the cake comes out clean.

3 Cool the cake in the pan for 20 minutes. Then invert onto a wire rack, and cool to room temperature. Transfer to a serving plate, sift the confectioners' sugar over the top, slice, and serve.

CINNAMON CARROT CAKE

Yield: 16 servings

2-1/2 cups unbleached flour

1-1/4 cups brown sugar

2 teaspoons baking soda

2 teaspoons ground cinnamon

3/4 cup plus 2 tablespoons apple juice

4 egg whites

2 teaspoons vanilla extract

3 cups grated carrots (about 6 medium)

1/3 cup dark raisins or chopped walnuts

Cream Cheese Icing:

8 ounces nonfat cream cheese

1 cup nonfat ricotta cheese

1/2 cup confectioners' sugar

1 teaspoon vanilla extract

1 Combine the flour, brown sugar, baking soda, and cinnamon, and stir to mix well. Add the juice, egg whites, and vanilla extract, and stir to mix well. Stir in the carrots and the raisins or walnuts.

2 Coat a 9-x-13-inch pan with nonstick cooking spray. Spread the batter evenly in the pan, and bake at 325°F for 40 to 50 minutes, or just until a wooden toothpick inserted in the center of the cake comes out clean. Cool to room temperature.

3 To make the icing, place the cream cheese and ricotta in a food processor, and process until smooth. Add the confectioners' sugar and vanilla extract, and process to mix well.

4 Spread the icing over the cooled cake. Cut into squares and serve immediately or refrigerate.

PEACH DELIGHT CAKE

Yield: 8 servings

NUTRITIONAL FACTS
(PER SERVING)

CALORIES: 161

FAT: 0.3 G

PROTEIN: 3.3 G

CHOLESTEROL: 0 MG

SODIUM: 86 MG

FIBER: 2.6 G

CALCIUM: 12 MG

POTASSIUM: 212 MG

IRON: 1.1 MG

3/4 cup unbleached flour

1/2 cup whole wheat flour

1/2 cup sugar

3/4 teaspoon baking soda

1/8 teaspoon ground nutmeg

2/3 cup puréed fresh peaches

3/4 teaspoon vanilla extract

3 tablespoons fat-free egg substitute

2 cups sliced fresh peaches
(about 3 medium)

1/4 cup dark raisins or chopped pecans

1 Combine the flours, sugar, baking soda, and nutmeg, and stir to mix well. Stir in the puréed peaches, vanilla extract, and egg substitute. Fold in the sliced peaches and the raisins or pecans.

2 Coat an 8-inch square pan with nonstick cooking spray. Spread the batter evenly in the pan, and bake at 350°F for about 35 minutes, or just until a wooden toothpick inserted in the center of the cake comes out clean.

3 Cool the cake for at least 20 minutes. Cut into squares and serve warm or at room temperature.

BUSY DAY BANANA CAKE

Yield: 16 servings

NUTRITIONAL FACTS (PER SERVING)
CALORIES: 215
FAT: 0.3 G
PROTEIN: 6.8 G
CHOLESTEROL: 0 MG
SODIUM: 107 MG
FIBER: 0.9 G
CALCIUM: 186 MG
POTASSIUM: 133 MG
IRON: 1.3 MG

1-1/3 cups unbleached flour

1/2 cup sugar

1-1/2 teaspoons baking powder

1/4 teaspoon ground nutmeg

2/3 cup mashed very ripe banana
(about 1-1/2 large)

1/3 cup maple syrup

3 tablespoons fat-free egg substitute

Icing:

1 cup nonfat ricotta cheese

2 tablespoons maple syrup

1/2 teaspoon vanilla extract

1. Combine the flour, sugar, baking powder, and nutmeg, and stir to mix well. Add the remaining ingredients, and stir to mix.

2. Coat an 8-inch square pan with nonstick cooking spray. Spread the batter evenly in the pan, and bake at 325°F for about 30 minutes, or just until a wooden toothpick inserted in the center of the cake comes out clean. Cool the cake to room temperature.

3. To make the icing, place the ricotta cheese, maple syrup, and vanilla extract in a food processor, and process until smooth. Spread the icing evenly over the cake, cut into squares, and serve immediately or refrigerate.

SPICED PEAR CAKE

Yield: 8 servings

NUTRITIONAL FACTS
(PER SERVING)

CALORIES: 169

FAT: 0.4 G

PROTEIN: 3.4 G

CHOLESTEROL: 0 MG

SODIUM: 85 MG

FIBER: 2.7 G

CALCIUM: 15 MG

POTASSIUM: 245 MG

IRON: 1.1 MG

3/4 cup unbleached flour

1/2 cup whole wheat flour

1/2 cup sugar

3/4 teaspoon baking soda

3/4 teaspoon ground cinnamon

1/8 teaspoon ground nutmeg

1/2 cup pear nectar

3 tablespoons fat-free egg substitute

2-1/2 cups thinly sliced fresh pears
    (about 2-1/2 medium)

1/4 cup dark raisins

1 Combine the flours, sugar, baking soda, and spices, and stir to mix well. Stir in the pear nectar and egg substitute. Fold in the pear slices and raisins.

2 Coat an 8-inch square pan with nonstick cooking spray. Spread the batter evenly in the pan, and bake at 350°F for 25 to 30 minutes, or just until a wooden toothpick inserted in the center of the cake comes out clean.

3 Cool the cake for at least 20 minutes. Cut into squares and serve warm or at room temperature.

PEAR STREUSEL COFFEE CAKE

Yield: 8 servings

NUTRITIONAL FACTS
(PER SERVING)

CALORIES: 196

FAT: 1.5 G

PROTEIN: 4.2 G

CHOLESTEROL: 0 MG

SODIUM: 109 MG

FIBER: 3 G

CALCIUM: 27 MG

POTASSIUM: 297 MG

IRON: 1.9 MG

3/4 cup unbleached flour

3/4 cup whole wheat flour

1/3 cup sugar

1 teaspoon baking soda

1/4 teaspoon ground nutmeg

1/2 cup plus 1 tablespoon apple juice

1-1/2 cups finely chopped fresh pears (about 2 medium)

Topping:

3 tablespoons light brown sugar

2 tablespoons whole wheat flour

2 tablespoons quick-cooking oats

2 tablespoons finely chopped walnuts

2-1/2 teaspoons frozen apple juice concentrate, thawed

1 To make the topping, combine the brown sugar, flour, oats, and walnuts. Stir in the apple juice concentrate, and mix until moist and crumbly. Set aside.

2 Combine the flours, sugar, baking soda, and nutmeg, and stir to mix well. Stir in the apple juice and the chopped pear.

3 Coat an 8-inch round pan with nonstick cooking spray. Spread the batter evenly in the pan, and sprinkle with the topping. Bake at 350°F for about 25 minutes, or just until a wooden toothpick inserted in the center of the cake comes out clean.

4 Cool the cake for at least 20 minutes. Cut into wedges and serve warm or at room temperature.

FRESH COCONUT CAKE

Yield: 16 servings

NUTRITIONAL FACTS (PER SERVING)
CALORIES: 178
FAT: 1.9 G
PROTEIN: 2.7 G
CHOLESTEROL: 0 MG
SODIUM: 121 MG
FIBER: 1.1 G
CALCIUM: 16 MG
POTASSIUM: 94 MG
IRON: 1 MG

1-1/4 cups coconut water (use some skim milk if there is not enough coconut water)*

3/4 cup diced fresh coconut

2-1/4 cups unbleached flour

1-1/3 cups sugar

2 teaspoons baking powder

1 teaspoon baking soda

2 egg whites

1 teaspoon vanilla extract

1 teaspoon coconut-flavored extract

Glaze:

1 cup confectioners' sugar

4 teaspoons coconut water or skim milk

1 teaspoon coconut-flavored extract

2 tablespoons grated fresh coconut

1 Place the coconut water and diced coconut in a food processor or blender, and process until the coconut is finely shredded. Set aside.

2 Combine the flour, sugar, baking powder, and baking soda, and stir to mix well. Add the coconut mixture, egg whites, vanilla extract, and coconut extract, and stir to mix well.

3 Coat a 9-x-13-inch pan with nonstick cooking spray. Spread the batter evenly in the pan, and bake at 325°F for 35 to 40 minutes, or just until a wooden toothpick inserted in the center of the cake comes out clean. Cool to room temperature.

4 To make the glaze, combine the glaze ingredients, stirring until smooth. Spread the glaze over the cooled cake, cut into squares, and serve.

* Coconut water is the fat-free liquid found inside the fresh coconut.

PUTTING COCONUT IN PERSPECTIVE

Rich in saturated fat, coconut oil is usually avoided in heart-healthy diets. Does this mean that the meat of the coconut is also off limits? Not necessarily. While coconut does contain coconut oil (one cup of grated coconut contains about six teaspoons of oil), small amounts of coconut may be added to recipes, especially if the recipe contains little or no other fat.

For example, our recipe for Fresh Coconut Cake (see page 52) contains about 3-1/3 ounces of fresh coconut in the whole cake. This means that each serving contains less than a half-teaspoon of coconut oil. Notice that the cake contains no other added fats such as butter, margarine, or oil. Coconut milk—which is extracted from the meat of the coconut, and therefore contains coconut oil—is not used. Instead, coconut water, the fat-free liquid found inside the coconut, helps to moisten the cake. The final result? One serving of Fresh Coconut Cake contains only 1.9 grams of fat. Not a high price to pay for the exotic sweetness of fresh coconut!

When reducing the fat in your own recipes, try to decrease the amount of coconut used instead of totally eliminating this flavorful ingredient. For example, instead of thickly covering the frosting with coconut, sprinkle the coconut sparingly over the top or just around the edge of the cake. This will enhance appearance and flavor without adding too much fat. A teaspoonful of coconut-flavored extract added to batter will reduce the amount of coconut needed.

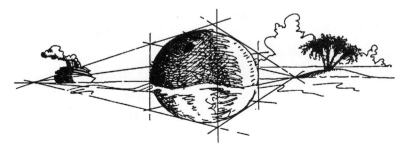

PEAR UPSIDE-DOWN CAKE

Yield: 10 servings

NUTRITIONAL FACTS (PER SERVING)	
CALORIES: 196	
FAT: 0.3 G	
PROTEIN: 3.3 G	
CHOLESTEROL: 0 MG	
SODIUM: 132 MG	
FIBER: 2.1 G	
CALCIUM: 23 MG	
POTASSIUM: 132 MG	
IRON: 1.4 MG	

2 cans (1 pound each) pear halves packed in juice, undrained
1/3 cup brown sugar
10 pecan halves (optional)
1 cup unbleached flour
2/3 cup whole wheat flour
1/3 cup sugar
1 teaspoon baking powder
1 teaspoon baking soda
1/3 cup honey or maple syrup
2 egg whites
1 teaspoon vanilla extract

1 Drain the pears, reserving the juice. Coat a 9-inch ovenproof skillet with nonstick cooking spray. Place 1-1/2 tablespoons of the reserved pear juice in the bottom of the skillet and distribute evenly. Sprinkle the brown sugar evenly over the pear juice. Arrange 10 pear halves over the brown sugar with the cut side down and the widest part of the pears toward the outer edge of the skillet. Fill in the center with pecan halves if desired.

2 Combine the flours, sugar, baking powder, and baking soda, and stir to mix well. Stir in 3/4 cup of the reserved pear juice and the honey or maple syrup, egg whites, and vanilla extract.

3 Pour the batter over the pears, spreading evenly. Bake at 350°F for 30 to 35 minutes, or just until a wooden toothpick inserted in the center of the cake comes out clean.

4 Let cool in the skillet for 15 minutes; then invert onto a serving platter. Cut into wedges and serve warm or at room temperature.

 PINEAPPLE DATE COFFEE CAKE

Yield: 9 servings

NUTRITIONAL FACTS
(PER SERVING)
CALORIES: 149
FAT: 0.9 G
PROTEIN: 3 G
CHOLESTEROL: 0 MG
SODIUM: 104 MG
FIBER: 3.2 G
CALCIUM: 27 MG
POTASSIUM: 218 MG
IRON: 1.3 MG

3/4 cup whole wheat flour

3/4 cup unbleached flour

1-1/2 teaspoons baking powder

1/2 teaspoon baking soda

1 can (8 ounces) crushed pineapple with juice, undrained

1/4 cup mashed very ripe banana (about 1/2 large)

1 teaspoon vanilla or almond extract

2/3 cup finely chopped dates

Topping:

1-1/2 tablespoons brown sugar

1-1/2 tablespoons shredded coconut

1. To make the topping, combine the sugar and coconut until crumbly. Set aside.

2. Combine the flours, baking powder, and baking soda, and stir to mix well. Stir in the pineapple (including the juice), banana, and vanilla or almond extract. Fold in the dates.

3. Coat an 8-inch square pan with nonstick cooking spray. Spread the batter evenly in the pan, and sprinkle with the topping. Bake at 325°F for 25 to 30 minutes, or just until a wooden toothpick inserted in the center of the cake comes out clean.

4. Cool the cake for at least 20 minutes. Cut into squares and serve warm or at room temperature.

COCOA STREUSEL CAKE

Yield: 16 servings

NUTRITIONAL FACTS
(PER SERVING)

CALORIES:	188
FAT:	1.1 G
PROTEIN:	3.5 G
CHOLESTEROL:	0 MG
SODIUM:	133 MG
FIBER:	2.8 G
CALCIUM:	29 MG
POTASSIUM:	129 MG
IRON:	1.4 MG

1 cup unbleached flour

3/4 cup whole wheat flour

1-1/4 cups sugar

1/3 cup cocoa powder

2 teaspoons baking soda

1-1/2 cups unsweetened applesauce

3/4 cup skim milk

2 teaspoons vanilla extract

Topping:

1-1/2 cups quick-cooking oats

1/4 cup unbleached flour

1/4 cup brown sugar

1/4 cup chocolate syrup

1. To make the topping, combine the oats, flour, and brown sugar. Add the chocolate syrup, and stir until the mixture is moist and crumbly. Set aside.

2. Combine the flours, sugar, cocoa, and baking soda, and stir to mix well. Add the applesauce, milk, and vanilla extract, and stir to mix well.

3. Coat a 9-x-13-inch pan with nonstick cooking spray. Spread the batter evenly in the pan, and sprinkle with the topping. Bake at 325°F for about 50 minutes, or just until a wooden toothpick inserted in the center of the cake comes out clean.

4. Cool the cake to room temperature, cut into squares, and serve.

OATMEAL FUDGE SQUARES

Yield: 16 servings

NUTRITIONAL FACTS (PER SERVING)	
CALORIES: 64	
FAT: 0.5 G	
PROTEIN: 1.4 G	
CHOLESTEROL: 0 MG	
SODIUM: 20 MG	
FIBER: 1 G	
CALCIUM: 5 MG	
POTASSIUM: 35 MG	
IRON: 0.4 MG	

1/2 cup plus 2 tablespoons quick-cooking oats

1/4 cup unsweetened applesauce or mashed banana

1/2 cup sugar

1/3 cup cocoa powder

2 tablespoons unbleached flour

1/4 teaspoon salt (optional)

1/4 cup honey

2 egg whites

1 teaspoon vanilla extract

1/4 cup chopped walnuts (optional)

1. Combine the oats and applesauce or banana, and let sit for 5 minutes. Add the remaining ingredients, and stir to mix well.

2. Coat an 8-inch square pan with nonstick cooking spray. Spread the batter evenly in the pan, and bake at 325°F for about 22 minutes, or just until the edges are firm and the center is almost set.

3. Cool to room temperature, cut into squares, and serve.

-FREE FUDGE BROWNIES

Yield: 16 servings

NUTRITIONAL FACTS (PER SERVING)
CALORIES: 80
FAT: 0.4 G
PROTEIN: 1.6 G
CHOLESTEROL: 0 MG
SODIUM: 25 MG
FIBER: 0.8 G
CALCIUM: 4 MG
POTASSIUM: 32 MG
IRON: 0.5 MG

3/4 cup unbleached flour

1/4 cup plus 2 tablespoons cocoa powder

1 cup sugar

1/4 teaspoon salt (optional)

1/3 cup unsweetened applesauce

3 egg whites

1 teaspoon vanilla extract

1/4 cup chopped walnuts (optional)

1 Combine the flour, cocoa, sugar, and salt, if desired, and stir to mix well. Stir in the applesauce, egg whites, and vanilla extract. Fold in the nuts if desired.

2 Coat an 8-inch square pan with nonstick cooking spray. Spread the batter evenly in the pan, and bake at 325°F for 23 to 25 minutes, or just until the edges are firm and the center is almost set.

3 Cool to room temperature, cut into squares, and serve.

COCOA BANANA BROWNIES

Yield: 16 servings

NUTRITIONAL FACTS
(PER SERVING)

CALORIES: 80

FAT: 0.8 G

PROTEIN: 2.1 G

CHOLESTEROL: 0 MG

SODIUM: 23 MG

FIBER: 1.7 G

CALCIUM: 7 MG

POTASSIUM: 96 MG

IRON: 0.5 MG

1 cup oat bran

1/3 cup cocoa powder

1 cup sugar

3/4 cup mashed very ripe banana
   (about 1 1/2 large)

3 egg whites

1 teaspoon vanilla extract

1/4 cup chopped walnuts (optional)

1 Combine the oat bran, cocoa, and sugar, and stir to mix well. Stir in the remaining ingredients.

2 Coat an 8-inch square pan with nonstick cooking spray. Spread the batter evenly in the pan, and bake at 325°F for 25 to 30 minutes, or just until the edges are firm and the center is almost set.

3 Cool to room temperature, cut into squares, and serve.

APPLESAUCE OATMEAL COOKIES

Yield: 50 cookies

NUTRITIONAL FACTS
(PER COOKIE)

CALORIES: 49

FAT: 0.3 G

PROTEIN: 1.2 G

CHOLESTEROL: 0 MG

SODIUM: 17 MG

FIBER: 1 G

CALCIUM: 5 MG

POTASSIUM: 48 MG

IRON: 0.4 MG

3 cups quick-cooking oats

1 cup whole wheat flour

1 teaspoon baking soda

1/4 teaspoon ground nutmeg

1 cup unsweetened applesauce

1 cup sugar

1 teaspoon vanilla extract

2/3 cup dark raisins

1 Combine the oats, flour, baking soda, and nutmeg, and stir to mix well. Add the applesauce, sugar, and vanilla extract, and stir to mix well. Stir in the raisins.

2 Coat cookie sheets with nonstick cooking spray. Roll the dough into 1-inch balls, and place the balls 1-1/2 inches apart on the cookie sheets. (If the dough is too sticky to handle, place it in the freezer for a few minutes.) Using the bottom of a glass dipped in sugar, flatten the cookies to 1/4-inch thickness.

3 Bake at 275°F for about 22 minutes, or until lightly browned. Transfer the cookies to wire racks, and cool completely. Serve immediately, or transfer to an airtight container and arrange in single layers separated by sheets of waxed paper.

WEST INDIAN BREAD PUDDING

Yield: 9 servings

NUTRITIONAL FACTS (PER SERVING)
CALORIES: 182
FAT: 0.8 G
PROTEIN: 6.3 G
CHOLESTEROL: 0 MG
SODIUM: 185 MG
FIBER: 1.2 G
CALCIUM: 72 MG
POTASSIUM: 275 MG
IRON: 1.5 MG

5 cups French bread cubes
    (about 6 ounces)
1/3 cup golden raisins
1 cup mashed very ripe banana
    (about 2 large)
1/4 cup plus 2 tablespoons honey
1-1/4 cups skim milk
1 cup fat-free egg substitute
1/4 teaspoon ground nutmeg
1 teaspoon vanilla extract

1 Combine the bread cubes and raisins. In a separate bowl, combine the remaining ingredients, and pour over the bread cubes. Stir gently to mix, and let the mixture sit for 10 minutes.

2 Coat a 1-1/2-quart casserole dish with nonstick cooking spray. Spread the bread mixture evenly in the dish, and bake at 350°F for 50 to 60 minutes, or until a sharp knife inserted in the center comes out clean.

3 Let stand for 10 minutes. Serve warm, and refrigerate any leftovers.

3 DAIRY FAT SUBSTITUTES

onfat buttermilk, nonfat yogurt, and even skim milk can deliciously and nutritiously replace some or all of the fat in muffins, quick breads, scones, biscuits, brownies, cookies, and many cakes. Rich in calcium, potassium, and magnesium, dairy products impart moistness to baked goods without altering flavor.

Of course, many people today don't use dairy products, but plenty of alternatives are available. For instance, soy yogurt and soy buttermilk can be substituted for dairy buttermilk and yogurt, while rice beverages and nut milks can be used instead of dairy milk. Some of these ingredients can be purchased at health foods stores, and some can be made at home. To make soy buttermilk, simply place one tablespoon of vinegar or lemon juice in a one-cup measure, and fill to the one-cup mark with low-fat soy milk. To make nut milk, place one-quarter cup of blanched almonds, macadamia nuts, Brazil nuts, or other nuts in a blender along with two cups of water. Blend until creamy, chill, and shake before using. Yes, nut milk does contain some fat—about as much as whole cow's milk. But the fat is unsaturated and comes packaged with nutrients like vitamin E. And, of course, nut milk has far less fat than the butter, margarine, or oil it will be replacing.

GETTING THE FAT OUT

Below, you'll find guidelines that will help you replace the fats in your own favorite recipes. (For more helpful hints on modifying recipes, see the inset on page 22.) Then you'll find a variety of tempting recipes for muffins, cakes, cobblers, and other desserts made lighter and healthier with dairy fat substitutes.

CAKE, MUFFIN, AND QUICK BREAD RECIPES

▓ Replace all or part of the butter, margarine, or other solid shortening in cake, muffin, and quick bread recipes with half as much nonfat buttermilk, nonfat yogurt, or skim milk. If the recipe calls for oil, replace all or part of the oil with three-fourths as much fat substitute. Mix up the batter. If it seems too dry, add a little more fat substitute. Some recipes may need a one-for-one substitution.

▓ When eliminating all of the fat from a recipe, reduce the number of eggs by half, or substitute 1 egg white for each whole egg. In some recipes, you may be able to eliminate the eggs altogether by replacing each whole egg with 2 tablespoons of fat substitute or another liquid.

▓ To retain moistness, bake fat-free and fat-reduced cakes, muffins, and quick breads at a slightly lower-than-standard temperature. Bake muffins at 350°F. Bake quick breads and cakes at 325°F to 350°F. *Be careful not to overbake.* Bake just until a wooden toothpick inserted in the center comes out clean.

BISCUIT AND SCONE RECIPES

▓ Replace all or part of the butter, margarine, or other solid shortening in biscuit and scone recipes with half as much nonfat buttermilk or nonfat yogurt. If the recipe calls for oil, replace all or part of the oil with three-fourths as much nonfat buttermilk or nonfat yogurt.

▓ When eliminating all of the fat from a biscuit or scone recipe, reduce the number of eggs by half, or substitute 1 egg white for each whole egg.

▓ Bake fat-free biscuits and scones at 375°F.

BROWNIE RECIPES

▨ Replace all of the butter, margarine, or other solid shortening in brownie recipes with half as much nonfat buttermilk or nonfat yogurt. If the recipe calls for oil, replace all of the oil with three-fourths as much fat substitute. Mix up the batter. If it seems too dry, add a bit more fat substitute. In some recipes—especially those made with oil—you will have to replace the fat with an equal amount of the dairy substitute.

▨ When eliminating all of the fat from a brownie recipe, you may replace each whole egg with 3 tablespoons of fat-free egg substitute if desired. However, it is not necessary to reduce the number of eggs.

▨ Bake fat-free brownies at 325°F, and check for doneness a few minutes before the end of the usual baking time. Remove the brownies from the oven as soon as the edges are firm and the center is almost set.

COOKIE RECIPES

▨ Replace half of the butter, margarine, or other solid shortening in cookie recipes with half as much nonfat buttermilk or nonfat yogurt. For example, if the recipe calls for 1 cup of butter, use 1/2 cup of butter and 1/4 cup of the chosen fat substitute. If the recipe calls for oil, replace half of the oil with three-fourths as much fat substitute. (You can replace more than half the fat, but the cookies may take on a cakey texture. Cookies that contain a high proportion of oats or oat bran are the easiest to make fat-free.)

▨ When reducing the fat in a cookie recipe, you may replace each whole egg with 3 tablespoons of fat-free egg substitute if desired. However, it is not necessary to reduce the number of eggs.

▨ Bake reduced-fat cookies at 275°F to 300°F.

APRICOT BRAN MUFFINS

Yield: 12 muffins

NUTRITIONAL FACTS
(PER MUFFIN)

CALORIES: 112

FAT: 0.6 G

PROTEIN: 4.4 G

CHOLESTEROL: 0 MG

SODIUM: 108 MG

FIBER: 4 G

CALCIUM: 49 MG

POTASSIUM: 346 MG

IRON: 1.9 MG

1-1/2 cups wheat bran
1-1/4 cups nonfat buttermilk
1 cup whole wheat flour
1 teaspoon baking soda
1/3 cup brown sugar
2 egg whites
1 cup chopped dried apricots

1. Combine the bran and buttermilk, and set aside for 15 minutes.

2. Combine the flour, baking soda, and brown sugar, and stir to mix well. Add the bran mixture and the egg whites, and stir just until the dry ingredients are moistened. Fold in the apricots.

3. Coat muffin cups with nonstick cooking spray, and fill 3/4 full with the batter. Bake at 350°F for 16 to 18 minutes, or just until a wooden toothpick inserted in the center of a muffin comes out clean.

4. Remove the muffin tin from the oven, and allow it to sit for 5 minutes before removing the muffins. Serve warm or at room temperature.

APPLE DATE MUFFINS

Yield: 12 muffins

NUTRITIONAL FACTS
(PER MUFFIN)
CALORIES: 135
FAT: 0.6 G
PROTEIN: 4.1 G
CHOLESTEROL: 0 MG
SODIUM: 129 MG
FIBER: 3.7 G
CALCIUM: 36 MG
POTASSIUM: 202 MG
IRON: 1.3 MG

2-1/4 cups whole wheat flour

1-1/2 teaspoons baking soda

1/3 cup brown sugar

3/4 cup nonfat buttermilk

1-1/2 cups finely chopped fresh apples
(about 2 medium)

3 tablespoons fat-free egg substitute

1 teaspoon vanilla extract

1/2 cup chopped dates

1. Combine the flour, baking soda, and brown sugar, and stir to mix well. Add the buttermilk, apple, egg substitute, and vanilla extract, and stir just until the dry ingredients are moistened. Fold in the dates.

2. Coat muffin cups with nonstick cooking spray, and fill 3/4 full with the batter. Bake at 350°F for 16 to 18 minutes, or just until a wooden toothpick inserted in the center of a muffin comes out clean.

3. Remove the muffin tin from the oven, and allow it to sit for 5 minutes before removing the muffins. Serve warm or at room temperature.

PLUM DELICIOUS BRAN MUFFINS

Yield: 12 muffins

NUTRITIONAL FACTS (PER MUFFIN)
CALORIES: 123
FAT: 0.7 G
PROTEIN: 3.7 G
CHOLESTEROL: 0 MG
SODIUM: 138 MG
FIBER: 3.3 G
CALCIUM: 40 MG
POTASSIUM: 221 MG
IRON: 1.1 MG

1-1/2 cups whole wheat flour

1/2 cup wheat bran or oat bran

1 tablespoon baking powder

1/2 teaspoon baking soda

3/4 cup apple butter

1/2 cup nonfat buttermilk or plain nonfat yogurt

2 egg whites

1 cup chopped skinned fresh plums (about 2 medium)

1/2 cup chopped prunes

1. Combine the flour, bran, baking powder, and baking soda, and stir to mix well. Add the apple butter, buttermilk or yogurt, and egg whites, and stir just until the dry ingredients are moistened. Fold in the plums and prunes.

2. Coat muffin cups with nonstick cooking spray, and fill 3/4 full with the batter. Bake at 350°F for 16 to 18 minutes, or just until a wooden toothpick inserted in the center of a muffin comes out clean.

3. Remove the muffin tin from the oven, and allow it to sit for 5 minutes before removing the muffins. Serve warm or at room temperature.

POPPY SEED MUFFINS

Yield: 10 muffins

NUTRITIONAL FACTS
(PER MUFFIN)

CALORIES: 106

FAT: 0.9 G

PROTEIN: 4.4 G

CHOLESTEROL: 0 MG

SODIUM: 107 MG

FIBER: 2.2 G

CALCIUM: 54 MG

POTASSIUM: 128 MG

IRON: 0.8 MG

1 cup whole wheat flour

1/2 cup oat flour

1/3 cup sugar

3–4 teaspoons poppy seeds

1 teaspoon baking soda

3/4 cup plain nonfat yogurt

2 egg whites

1 teaspoon vanilla or almond extract

1/4 cup chopped almonds (optional)

1 Combine the flours, sugar, poppy seeds, and baking soda, and stir to mix well. Add the yogurt, egg whites, and vanilla or almond extract, and stir just until the dry ingredients are moistened. Fold in the almonds if desired.

2 Coat muffin cups with nonstick cooking spray, and fill 3/4 full with the batter. Bake at 350°F for 14 to 16 minutes, or just until a wooden toothpick inserted in the center of a muffin comes out clean.

3 Remove the muffin tin from the oven, and allow it to sit for 5 minutes before removing the muffins. Serve warm or at room temperature.

BLUEBERRY BRAN MUFFINS

Yield: 12 muffins

NUTRITIONAL FACTS
(PER MUFFIN)

CALORIES: 106

FAT: 0.9 G

PROTEIN: 4.2 G

CHOLESTEROL: 0 MG

SODIUM: 145 MG

FIBER: 2.9 G

CALCIUM: 47 MG

POTASSIUM: 138 MG

IRON: 0.8 MG

1-1/4 cups whole wheat flour

3/4 cup oat bran or wheat bran

1/3 cup sugar

1 teaspoon baking soda

2 teaspoons baking powder

1 cup vanilla or lemon nonfat yogurt

2 egg whites

1 teaspoon vanilla extract

3/4 cup fresh or frozen blueberries

1 Combine the flour, bran, sugar, baking soda, and baking powder, and stir to mix well. Add the yogurt, egg whites, and vanilla extract, and stir just until the dry ingredients are moistened. Fold in the blueberries.

2 Coat muffin cups with nonstick cooking spray, and fill 3/4 full with the batter. Bake at 350°F for 16 to 18 minutes, or just until a wooden toothpick inserted in the center of a muffin comes out clean.

3 Remove the muffin tin from the oven, and allow it to sit for 5 minutes before removing the muffins. Serve warm or at room temperature.

CHERRY WALNUT MUFFINS

Yield: 12 muffins

NUTRITIONAL FACTS (PER MUFFIN)
CALORIES: 137
FAT: 0.8 G
PROTEIN: 4.4 G
CHOLESTEROL: 0 MG
SODIUM: 148 MG
FIBER: 2.2 G
CALCIUM: 56 MG
POTASSIUM: 164 MG
IRON: 0.8 MG

1-1/2 cups whole wheat flour

1/2 cup brown rice flour or whole grain cornmeal

1/2 cup sugar

2 teaspoons baking powder

1 teaspoon baking soda

1 cup plain nonfat yogurt

1-1/2 teaspoons vanilla extract

2 egg whites

3/4 cup coarsely chopped frozen pitted cherries

Topping:

1 tablespoon sugar

1 tablespoon finely ground walnuts

1 To make the topping, combine the sugar and walnuts until crumbly. Set aside.

2 Combine the whole wheat flour, rice flour or cornmeal, sugar, baking powder, and baking soda, and stir to mix well. Add the yogurt, vanilla extract, and egg whites, and stir just until the dry ingredients are moistened. Fold in the cherries.

3 Coat muffin cups with nonstick cooking spray, and fill 3/4 full with the batter. Sprinkle the topping over the batter. Bake at 350°F for 15 to 18 minutes, or just until a wooden toothpick inserted in the center of a muffin comes out clean.

4 Remove the muffin tin from the oven, and allow it to sit for 5 minutes before removing the muffins. Serve warm or at room temperature.

BANANA GRANOLA MUFFINS

Yield: 12 muffins

NUTRITIONAL FACTS
(PER MUFFIN)

CALORIES: 150

FAT: 0.5 G

PROTEIN: 5 G

CHOLESTEROL: 0 MG

SODIUM: 195 MG

FIBER: 3.5 G

CALCIUM: 42 MG

POTASSIUM: 211 MG

IRON: 1.5 MG

1-1/3 cups whole wheat flour

1 tablespoon baking powder

3/4 cup mashed very ripe banana
   (about 1-1/2 large)

1/2 cup skim milk

1/4 cup maple syrup or honey

2 egg whites

2 cups nonfat or low-fat granola cereal

Topping:

1/4 cup nonfat or low-fat granola cereal

1 Combine the flour and baking powder, and stir to mix well. Add the banana, skim milk, maple syrup or honey, and egg whites, and stir just until the dry ingredients are moistened. Stir in the 2 cups of granola.

2 Coat muffin cups with nonstick cooking spray, and fill 3/4 full with the batter. Sprinkle the topping over the muffins, and press lightly into the batter. Bake at 350°F for 14 to 16 minutes, or just until a wooden toothpick inserted in the center of a muffin comes out clean.

3 Remove the muffin tin from the oven, and allow it to sit for 5 minutes before removing the muffins. Serve warm or at room temperature.

CARROT SPICE MUFFINS

Yield: 12 muffins

NUTRITIONAL FACTS
(PER MUFFIN)

CALORIES: 119

FAT: 0.8 G

PROTEIN: 3.4 G

CHOLESTEROL: 0 MG

SODIUM: 145 MG

FIBER: 3.4 G

CALCIUM: 46 MG

POTASSIUM: 206 MG

IRON: 1.2 MG

2 cups whole wheat flour

2 teaspoons baking powder

1 teaspoon baking soda

3/4 teaspoon ground cinnamon

3/4 teaspoon ground nutmeg

1/3 cup maple syrup or honey

1/3 cup skim milk

2 egg whites

2 cups grated carrots (about 4 medium)

1/3 cup golden raisins or chopped pecans

1 Combine the flour, baking powder, baking soda, cinnamon, and nutmeg, and stir to mix well. Add the maple syrup or honey, skim milk, egg whites, and carrot, and stir just until the dry ingredients are moistened. Fold in the raisins or pecans.

2 Coat muffin cups with nonstick cooking spray, and fill 3/4 full with the batter. Bake at 350°F for 15 to 17 minutes, or just until a wooden toothpick inserted in the center of a muffin comes out clean.

3 Remove the muffin tin from the oven, and allow it to sit for 5 minutes before removing the muffins. Serve warm or at room temperature.

PINEAPPLE BRAN MUFFINS

Yield: 12 muffins

NUTRITIONAL FACTS
(PER MUFFIN)
CALORIES: 106
FAT: 0.6 G
PROTEIN: 4.8 G
CHOLESTEROL: 0 MG
SODIUM: 105 MG
FIBER: 4.7 G
CALCIUM: 60 MG
POTASSIUM: 224 MG
IRON: 1.4 MG

1-1/4 cups skim milk

1-1/2 cups wheat bran

1/2 cup date sugar or brown sugar

1-1/2 cups whole wheat flour

1 tablespoon baking powder

1 can (8 ounces) crushed pineapple packed in juice, undrained

2 egg whites

1/3 cup chopped pecans (optional)

1 Combine the milk, wheat bran, and date or brown sugar, and set aside for 15 minutes.

2 Combine the flour and baking powder, and stir to mix well. Add the bran mixture, the pineapple with its juice, and the egg whites, and stir just until the dry ingredients are moistened. Fold in the pecans if desired.

3 Coat muffin cups with nonstick cooking spray, and fill 3/4 full with the batter. Bake at 350°F for about 18 minutes, or just until a wooden toothpick inserted in the center of a muffin comes out clean.

4 Remove the muffin tin from the oven, and allow it to sit for 5 minutes before removing the muffins. Serve warm or at room temperature.

RISE-AND-SHINE MUFFINS

Yield: 12 muffins

NUTRITIONAL FACTS
(PER MUFFIN)

CALORIES: 135

FAT: 0.4 G

PROTEIN: 4.4 G

CHOLESTEROL: 0 MG

SODIUM: 180 MG

FIBER: 3.4 G

CALCIUM: 62 MG

POTASSIUM: 234 MG

IRON: 2.4 MG

2-1/4 cups bran flake-and-raisin cereal

1-1/3 cups skim milk

3 tablespoons fat-free egg substitute

1 teaspoon vanilla extract

1-1/2 cups whole wheat flour

1/2 cup sugar

1 tablespoon baking powder

1/4 teaspoon ground cinnamon

1/2 cup chopped dried apricots or prunes

1/4 cup hulled sunflower seeds (optional)

1 Combine the cereal, milk, egg substitute, and vanilla extract, and set aside for 10 minutes.

2 Combine the flour, sugar, baking powder, and cinnamon, and stir to mix well. Add the cereal mixture, and stir just until the dry ingredients are moistened. Fold in the apricots or prunes and the sunflower seeds if desired.

3 Coat muffin cups with nonstick cooking spray, and fill 3/4 full with the batter. Bake at 350°F for 16 to 18 minutes, or just until a wooden toothpick inserted in the center of a muffin comes out clean.

4 Remove the muffin tin from the oven, and allow it to sit for 5 minutes before removing the muffins. Serve warm or at room temperature.

GERMAN CHOCOLATE MUFFINS

Yield: 14 muffins

1-1/2 cups whole wheat flour

3/4 cup oat flour

1/4 cup cocoa powder

2/3 cup light brown sugar

1 tablespoon baking powder

1-1/2 cups nonfat buttermilk

2 egg whites

1-1/2 teaspoons vanilla extract

1 teaspoon coconut-flavored extract

Topping:

1 tablespoon shredded coconut

1 tablespoon light brown sugar

1. To make the topping, combine the coconut and brown sugar until crumbly. Set aside.

2. Combine the flours, cocoa, brown sugar, and baking powder, and stir to mix well. Add the buttermilk, egg whites, and extracts, and stir just until the dry ingredients are moistened.

3. Coat muffin cups with nonstick cooking spray, and fill 3/4 full with the batter. Sprinkle the topping over the batter. Bake at 350°F for 14 to 16 minutes, or just until a wooden toothpick inserted in the center of a muffin comes out clean.

4. Remove the muffin tin from the oven, and allow it to sit for 5 minutes before removing the muffins. Serve warm or at room temperature.

ANADAMA QUICK BREAD

Yield: 16 slices

NUTRITIONAL FACTS
(PER SLICE)

CALORIES: 100

FAT: 0.6 G

PROTEIN: 4 G

CHOLESTEROL: 0 MG

SODIUM: 128 MG

FIBER: 2.6 G

CALCIUM: 53 MG

POTASSIUM: 186 MG

IRON: 1.1 MG

2-1/3 cups whole wheat flour

1/2 cup whole grain cornmeal

2 teaspoons baking powder

1 teaspoon baking soda

1-1/2 cups plus 2 tablespoons nonfat buttermilk

1/3 cup molasses

2 egg whites, slightly beaten

1 Combine the flour, cornmeal, baking powder, and baking soda, and stir to mix well. Add the remaining ingredients, and stir just until the dry ingredients are moistened.

2 Coat an 8-x-4-inch loaf pan with nonstick cooking spray. Spread the mixture evenly in the pan, and bake at 350°F for about 45 minutes, or just until a wooden toothpick inserted in the center of the loaf comes out clean.

3 Remove the bread from the oven, and let sit for 10 minutes. Invert the loaf onto a wire rack, turn right side up, and cool before slicing and serving.

TWO-BRAN BREAKFAST BREAD

Yield: 16 slices

NUTRITIONAL FACTS (PER SLICE)	
CALORIES: 89	
FAT: 0.4 G	
PROTEIN: 3.1 G	
CHOLESTEROL: 0 MG	
SODIUM: 84 MG	
FIBER: 2.7 G	
CALCIUM: 41 MG	
POTASSIUM: 178 MG	
IRON: 0.9 MG	

1/4 cup wheat bran

1/3 cup orange juice

1-2/3 cups whole wheat flour

1/4 cup oat bran

1/3 cup sugar

1 teaspoon baking powder

1 teaspoon baking soda

1 cup plain nonfat yogurt

1/3 cup chopped dried apricots

1/3 cup chopped prunes

1 Combine the wheat bran and orange juice, and set aside for at least 5 minutes.

2 Combine the flour, oat bran, sugar, baking powder, and baking soda, and stir to mix well.

3 Add the wheat bran mixture and the yogurt to the flour mixture, and stir just until the dry ingredients are moistened. Fold in the apricots and prunes.

4 Coat an 8-x-4-inch loaf pan with nonstick cooking spray. Spread the mixture evenly in the pan, and bake at 350°F for 35 to 40 minutes, or just until a wooden toothpick inserted in the center of the loaf comes out clean.

5 Remove the bread from the oven, and let sit for 10 minutes. Invert the loaf onto a wire rack, turn right side up, and cool before slicing and serving.

BOSTON BANANA BROWN BREAD

Yield: 32 slices

NUTRITIONAL FACTS
(PER SLICE)
CALORIES: 74
FAT: 0.4 G
PROTEIN: 1.8 G
CHOLESTEROL: 0 MG
SODIUM: 36 MG
FIBER: 1.8 G
CALCIUM: 22 MG
POTASSIUM: 168 MG
IRON: 0.7 MG

2 cups whole wheat flour

1 cup whole grain cornmeal

1 teaspoon baking soda

1/4 teaspoon ground nutmeg

1-1/2 cups mashed very ripe banana
   (about 3 large)

1 cup nonfat buttermilk

1/2 cup molasses

3/4 cup chopped dried dates

1. Combine the flour, cornmeal, baking soda, and nutmeg, and stir to mix well. Add the banana, buttermilk, and molasses, and stir just until the dry ingredients are moistened. Fold in the dates.

2. Coat 4 one-pound cans with nonstick cooking spray. Divide the batter among the cans, and bake at 300°F for about 40 minutes, or just until a wooden toothpick inserted in the center of a loaf comes out clean.

3. Remove the bread from the oven, and let sit for 10 minutes. Invert the loaves onto a wire rack, turn right side up, and cool before slicing and serving.

REALLY RASPBERRY SCONES

Yield: 12 scones

NUTRITIONAL FACTS
(PER SCONE)

CALORIES: 112

FAT: 0.5 G

PROTEIN: 3.8 G

CHOLESTEROL: 0 MG

SODIUM: 104 MG

FIBER: 1.5 G

CALCIUM: 42 MG

POTASSIUM: 85 MG

IRON: 1.1 MG

1-1/2 cups unbleached flour

1 cup quick-cooking oats

2 tablespoons sugar

2 teaspoons baking powder

1/2 teaspoon baking soda

1 egg white

3/4 cup plus 2 tablespoons lemon or vanilla nonfat yogurt

1/2 cup chopped fresh or frozen raspberries

Skim milk or 1 beaten egg white

1 Combine the flour, oats, sugar, baking powder, and baking soda, and stir to mix well. Stir in the egg white and just enough of the yogurt to form a stiff dough. Gently stir in the raspberries.

2 Form the dough into a ball, and turn onto a lightly floured surface. With floured hands, pat the dough into a 7-inch circle.

3 Coat a baking sheet with nonstick cooking spray. Place the dough on the sheet, and use a sharp floured knife to cut it into 12 wedges. Pull the wedges out slightly to leave a 1/2-inch space between them. Brush the tops lightly with skim milk or beaten egg white.

4 Bake at 375°F for 20 minutes, or until lightly browned. Transfer to a serving plate, and serve hot with raspberry fruit spread.

PEAR AND WALNUT BUNDT CAKE

Yield: 16 servings

1-1/2 cups unbleached flour

1 cup whole wheat flour

1 cup brown sugar

2 teaspoons baking soda

1 cup apple butter

1/2 cup plain nonfat yogurt

2 egg whites

1 teaspoon vanilla extract

1 cup finely chopped fresh pears
    (about 1 medium)

1/3 cup chopped walnuts (optional)

Topping:

1/3 cup confectioners' sugar

1 tablespoon apple butter

1 tablespoon chopped walnuts

1 Combine the flours, brown sugar, and baking soda, and stir to mix well. Add the apple butter, yogurt, egg whites, and vanilla extract, and stir to mix well. Fold in the pears and walnuts.

2 Coat a 12-cup bundt pan with nonstick cooking spray. Spread the batter evenly in the pan, and bake at 325°F for 35 to 45 minutes, or just until a wooden toothpick inserted in the center of the cake comes out clean. Cool the cake in the pan for 20 minutes. Then invert onto a wire rack, and cool to room temperature.

3 To make the topping, combine the confectioners' sugar with the apple butter. Transfer the cake to a serving platter, and drizzle the topping over the cake. Sprinkle the walnuts over the glaze. Let sit for at least 15 minutes before slicing and serving.

BLUEBERRY SUNSHINE CAKE

Yield: 16 servings

NUTRITIONAL FACTS (PER SERVING)
CALORIES: 167
FAT: 0.9 G
PROTEIN: 3.5 G
CHOLESTEROL: 0 MG
SODIUM: 83 MG
FIBER: 1.4 G
CALCIUM: 26 MG
POTASSIUM: 104 MG
IRON: 1.1 MG

2-1/3 cups unbleached flour

2/3 cup oat bran

1-1/4 cups sugar

1 tablespoon plus 1-1/2 teaspoons lecithin granules*

1-1/4 teaspoons baking soda

2 teaspoons dried grated orange rind, or 2 tablespoons fresh

1 cup orange juice

1/2 cup nonfat buttermilk

2 egg whites

3/4 cup fresh or frozen blueberries

Glaze:

1/3 cup confectioners' sugar

2-1/2 teaspoons frozen orange juice concentrate, thawed

1 Combine the flour, oat bran, sugar, lecithin, baking soda, and orange rind, and stir to mix well. Add the orange juice, buttermilk, and egg whites, and stir to mix well. Fold in the blueberries.

2 Coat a 12-cup bundt pan with nonstick cooking spray. Spread the batter evenly in the pan, and bake at 350°F for 35 to 45 minutes, or just until a wooden toothpick inserted in the center of the cake comes out clean. Cool the cake in the pan for 20 minutes. Then invert onto a wire rack, and cool to room temperature.

3 To make the glaze, combine the confectioners' sugar with the juice concentrate. Transfer the cake to a serving platter, and drizzle the glaze over the cake. Let sit for at least 15 minutes before slicing and serving.

* For information on lecithin, see the inset on page 83.

LECITHIN—A LITTLE BIT GOES A LONG WAY

Lecithin, a nutritious by-product of soybean-oil refining, is a perfect texture enhancer for fat-free baked goods. In fact, commercial bakers frequently use small amounts of lecithin in very low-fat and fat-free cakes, cookies, and other baked goods. Lecithin's unique chemical properties allow batters to rise better, and lend a softer texture to the finished product.

Lecithin is available in both liquid and granular forms. Both forms can be found in health foods stores, where lecithin is sold as a nutritional supplement. Lecithin liquid is very thick and sticky—so sticky that it's almost impossible to work with. Lecithin granules, however, are puffed-up bits of oil that are easily measured and added to batters. Because the granules are puffed, though, they cannot be substituted for the liquid on a measure-for-measure basis. The recipes in this book call for lecithin granules. If you use the liquid form, use half as much. Regardless of the form you choose to use, keep your lecithin in the refrigerator to maintain freshness.

Lecithin granules do contain fat—6 grams per tablespoon. The liquid has 12 grams of fat per tablespoon because it is more dense. Unlike many fat-rich ingredients, though, lecithin is also rich in nutrients, especially vitamin E, iron, phosphorus, calcium, and choline, a nutrient that people on low-fat diets may not get enough of. Added in small amounts to a recipe, lecithin raises the fat content only slightly. For instance, most of the bundt cakes in this chapter contain 1-1/2 tablespoons of lecithin. This adds 9 grams of fat to the whole recipe, or about 0.5 grams per serving. The improvement in texture is well worth the price. In fact, a tablespoon or two of lecithin granules may be added to any recipe in this book for an extra soft and velvety texture that you and your family will love.

BLUEBERRY LEMON TUNNEL CAKE

Yield: 16 servings

NUTRITIONAL FACTS
(PER SERVING)

CALORIES: 179	
FAT: 1 G	
PROTEIN: 3.8 G	
CHOLESTEROL: 0 MG	
SODIUM: 114 MG	
FIBER: 1.5 G	
CALCIUM: 40 MG	
POTASSIUM: 103 MG	
IRON: 1.2 MG	

For variety, substitute lemon or cherry pie filling for the blueberry filling.

2-1/4 cups unbleached flour

3/4 cup oat bran

1-1/4 cups sugar

1 tablespoon plus 1-1/2 teaspoons lecithin granules*

1-1/2 teaspoons baking soda

1 teaspoon dried grated lemon rind, or 1 tablespoon fresh

1-1/2 cups nonfat buttermilk

2 egg whites

1-1/2 teaspoons vanilla extract

Filling:

1-1/4 cups canned blueberry pie filling

Glaze:

1/3 cup confectioners' sugar

1-3/4 teaspoons lemon juice

1 Combine the flour, oat bran, sugar, lecithin, baking soda, and lemon rind, and stir to mix well. Add the buttermilk, egg whites, and vanilla extract, and stir to mix well.

2 Coat a 12-cup bundt pan with nonstick cooking spray. Spread the batter evenly in the pan. Spoon the filling in a ring over the center of the batter. (The filling will sink into the batter as the cake bakes.)

3 Bake at 350°F for about 40 minutes, or until the top springs back when lightly touched, and a wooden toothpick inserted near the side comes out clean. Cool the cake in the pan for 40 minutes. Then invert onto a wire rack, and cool to room temperature.

4 To make the glaze, combine the confectioners' sugar with the lemon juice. Transfer the cake to a serving platter, and spoon the glaze over the cake. Let sit for at least 15 minutes before slicing and serving.

* For information on lecithin, see the inset on page 83.

WHITE CAKE WITH STRAWBERRIES

Yield: 8 servings

NUTRITIONAL FACTS (PER SERVING)
CALORIES: 152
FAT: 0.6 G
PROTEIN: 3.3 G
CHOLESTEROL: 0 MG
SODIUM: 121 MG
FIBER: 0.5 G
CALCIUM: 43 MG
POTASSIUM: 179 MG
IRON: 1.1 MG

1 cup plus 2 tablespoons unbleached flour

1/2 cup sugar

1 teaspoon baking powder

1/2 teaspoon baking soda

1/2 cup plus 2 tablespoons nonfat
    buttermilk

1 egg white

1 teaspoon vanilla extract

Topping:

4 cups sliced fresh strawberries

2 tablespoons sugar

1 tablespoon amaretto liqueur

1 Combine the topping ingredients. Cover and chill for several hours or overnight.

2 Combine the flour, sugar, baking powder, and baking soda, and stir to mix well. Stir in the buttermilk, egg white, and vanilla extract.

3 Coat a 9-inch round pan with nonstick cooking spray. Spread the batter evenly in the pan, and bake at 325°F for 15 to 20 minutes, or just until the center springs back when lightly touched and a wooden toothpick inserted in the center of the cake comes out clean.

4 Cool the cake to room temperature. Cut into wedges, top each serving with the strawberry mixture, and serve.

BANANA FUDGE RIPPLE CAKE

Yield: 16 servings

NUTRITIONAL FACTS
(PER SERVING)
CALORIES: 170
FAT: 1.1 G
PROTEIN: 3.5 G
CHOLESTEROL: 0 MG
SODIUM: 87 MG
FIBER: 1.7 G
CALCIUM: 25 MG
POTASSIUM: 161 MG
IRON: 1.2 MG

2 cups unbleached flour

3/4 cup oat bran

1-1/4 cups sugar

1 tablespoon plus 1-1/2 teaspoons lecithin granules*

1-1/4 teaspoons baking soda

1-1/2 cups mashed very ripe banana (about 3 large)

1/2 cup nonfat buttermilk

2 egg whites

1-1/2 teaspoons vanilla extract

1/3 cup chocolate syrup

1-1/2 tablespoons confectioners' sugar

1 Combine the flour, oat bran, sugar, lecithin, and baking soda, and stir to mix well. Add the banana, buttermilk, egg whites, and vanilla extract, and stir to mix well. Remove 1/3 cup of the batter and mix with the chocolate syrup.

2 Coat a 12-cup bundt pan with nonstick cooking spray. Spread 1/3 of the plain batter evenly in the pan, top with half of the chocolate mixture, add another 1/3 of the batter, top with the remaining chocolate mixture, and finish with the rest of the batter.

3 Bake at 350°F for about 40 minutes, or just until a wooden tooth-pick inserted in the center of the cake comes out clean. Cool the cake in the pan for 20 minutes. Then invert onto a wire rack, and cool to room temperature.

4 Transfer the cake to a serving platter. Sift the confectioners' sugar over the cooled cake, slice, and serve.

* For information on lecithin, see the inset on page 83.

CHERRY ALMOND CAKE

Yield: 16 servings

NUTRITIONAL FACTS	
(PER SERVING)	
CALORIES: 165	
FAT: 0.7 G	
PROTEIN: 2.4 G	
CHOLESTEROL: 0 MG	
SODIUM: 111 MG	
FIBER: 1.4 G	
CALCIUM: 34 MG	
POTASSIUM: 46 MG	
IRON: 1 MG	

For a change of pace, use blueberry, peach, or raspberry pie filling instead of the cherry filling.

2-1/4 cups unbleached flour

1-1/4 cups sugar

1 tablespoon lecithin granules*

2 teaspoons baking powder

1 teaspoon baking soda

1 cup plus 2 tablespoons nonfat buttermilk

2 egg whites

1 teaspoon vanilla extract

1 teaspoon almond extract

1 can (20 ounces) light (low-sugar) cherry pie filling

1 Combine the flour, sugar, lecithin, baking powder, and baking soda, and stir to mix well. Add the buttermilk, egg whites, vanilla extract, and almond extract, and stir to mix well.

2 Coat a 9-x-13-inch pan with nonstick cooking spray. Spread the batter evenly in the pan. Spoon the cherry filling back and forth over the cake in an "S" pattern. (The filling will sink into the batter as the cake bakes.)

3 Bake at 325°F for 45 to 50 minutes, or just until a wooden toothpick inserted in the center of the cake comes out clean. (Find a spot that is free of cherry filling.)

4 Cool the cake for at least 20 minutes. Cut into squares and serve warm or at room temperature.

* For information on lecithin, see the inset on page 83.

COCOA MARBLE BUNDT CAKE

Yield: 16 servings

NUTRITIONAL FACTS
(PER SERVING)

CALORIES: 174

FAT: 1.3 G

PROTEIN: 4.1 G

CHOLESTEROL: 0 MG

SODIUM: 112 MG

FIBER: 1.9 G

CALCIUM: 35 MG

POTASSIUM: 106 MG

IRON: 1.4 MG

2-1/4 cups unbleached flour

3/4 cup oat bran

1-1/3 cups sugar

1 tablespoon plus 1-1/2 teaspoons lecithin granules*

1-1/4 teaspoons baking soda

1-2/3 cups nonfat buttermilk

2 egg whites

1-1/2 teaspoons vanilla extract

1/4 cup chocolate syrup

1/4 cup cocoa powder

Glaze:

1/3 cup confectioners' sugar

1 tablespoon cocoa powder

2 teaspoons skim milk

1/2 teaspoon vanilla extract

1 Combine the flour, oat bran, sugar, lecithin, and baking soda, and stir to mix well. Add the buttermilk, egg whites, and vanilla extract, and stir to mix well. Remove 1 cup of the batter and mix with the chocolate syrup and cocoa powder.

2 Coat a 12-cup bundt pan with nonstick cooking spray. Spread 3/4 of the plain batter evenly in the pan, top with the chocolate mixture, and add the remaining batter.

3 Bake at 350°F for 35 to 45 minutes, or just until a wooden toothpick inserted in the center of the cake comes out clean. Cool the cake in the pan for 20 minutes. Then invert onto a wire rack, and cool to room temperature.

Top: Banana Granola Muffins (page 72)
Bottom Left: Poppy Seed Muffins (page 69)
Bottom Right: German Chocolate Muffins (page 76)

Top: *White Cake With Strawberries (page 85)*
Bottom: *Blueberry Sunshine Cake (page 82)*

Top: Very Berry Cobbler (page 98)
Bottom: Blueberry Lemon Streusel Cake (page 90)

4 To make the glaze, combine the glaze ingredients, stirring until smooth. Transfer the cake to a serving platter, and drizzle the glaze over the cake. Let sit for at least 15 minutes before slicing and serving.

* For information on lecithin, see the inset on page 83.

*B*UTTERMILK CHOCOLATE CAKE

Yield: 16 servings

NUTRITIONAL FACTS (PER SERVING)
CALORIES: 156
FAT: 1.3 G
PROTEIN: 2.9 G
CHOLESTEROL: 0 MG
SODIUM: 136 MG
FIBER: 1.4 G
CALCIUM: 56 MG
POTASSIUM: 70 MG
IRON: 1.1 MG

1-1/2 cups unbleached flour
1/2 cup oat flour
1-1/2 cups sugar
1/2 cup plus 1 tablespoon cocoa powder
2 teaspoons baking soda
1-1/2 cups nonfat buttermilk
1/4 cup water
2 teaspoons vanilla extract

Frosting:

1 tablespoon cocoa powder
1 cup nonfat vanilla yogurt
1 cup light whipped topping

1 Combine the flours, sugar, cocoa, and baking soda, and stir to mix well. Stir in the buttermilk, water, and vanilla extract.

2 Coat a 9-x-13-inch pan with nonstick cooking spray. Spread the batter evenly in the pan, and bake at 350°F for 30 to 35 minutes, or until a wooden toothpick inserted in the center of the cake comes out clean. Cool the cake to room temperature.

3 To make the frosting, stir the cocoa into the yogurt. Then gently fold the yogurt into the whipped topping. Spread the frosting evenly over the cake, cut into squares, and serve immediately or refrigerate.

BLUEBERRY LEMON STREUSEL CAKE

Yield: 9 servings

NUTRITIONAL FACTS
(PER SERVING)

CALORIES: 184	
FAT: 0.9 G	
PROTEIN: 5 G	
CHOLESTEROL: 0 MG	
SODIUM: 164 MG	
FIBER: 2.3 G	
CALCIUM: 58 MG	
POTASSIUM: 124 MG	
IRON: 1.5 MG	

2/3 cup skim milk

2 tablespoons lemon juice

1-1/2 cups unbleached flour

1/2 cup oat flour

1/2 cup sugar

4 teaspoons baking powder

1 teaspoon dried grated lemon rind, or
   1 tablespoon fresh

1 egg white

1-1/2 cups fresh or frozen blueberries

Topping:

1/4 cup quick-cooking oats

1 tablespoon toasted wheat germ

1/8 teaspoon ground nutmeg

2 teaspoons honey

1. To make the topping, combine the oats, wheat germ, and nutmeg. Stir in the honey until the mixture is moist and crumbly. Set aside.

2. Combine the milk and lemon juice, and set aside for 2 minutes.

3. Combine the flours, sugar, baking powder, and lemon rind, and stir to mix well. Stir in the lemon juice mixture and the egg white. Fold in the blueberries.

4. Coat an 8-inch square pan with nonstick cooking spray. Spread the batter evenly in the pan, and sprinkle with the topping.

5. Bake at 350°F for 35 to 40 minutes, or until a wooden toothpick inserted in the center of the cake comes out clean.

6 Cool the cake for at least 20 minutes. Cut into squares and serve warm or at room temperature.

CINNAMON NUT COFFEE CAKE

Yield: 9 servings

NUTRITIONAL FACTS
(PER SERVING)
CALORIES: 172
FAT: 1.9 G
PROTEIN: 3.6 G
CHOLESTEROL: 0 MG
SODIUM: 148 MG
FIBER: 1.6 G
CALCIUM: 51 MG
POTASSIUM: 147 MG
IRON: 1.6 MG

1 cup unbleached flour

1/2 cup whole wheat flour

2 teaspoons baking powder

1/2 teaspoon baking soda

2/3 cup light brown sugar

1/2 cup unsweetened applesauce

1/2 cup nonfat buttermilk

3 tablespoons fat-free egg substitute

1 teaspoon vanilla extract

Topping:

18 pecan halves

4-1/2 teaspoons sugar

3/4 teaspoon ground cinnamon

1 Combine the flours, baking powder, baking soda, and brown sugar, and stir to mix well. Add the applesauce, buttermilk, egg substitute, and vanilla extract, and stir to mix well.

2 Coat an 8-inch square pan with nonstick cooking spray. Spread the batter evenly in the pan. Arrange the pecan halves on top of the batter, pressing each nut slightly into the batter. Combine the sugar and cinnamon, and sprinkle over the top.

3 Bake at 350°F for about 25 minutes, or just until a wooden toothpick inserted in the center of the cake comes out clean.

4 Cool the cake for at least 20 minutes. Cut into squares and serve warm or at room temperature.

ℬERRY DELICIOUS CRUMB CAKE

Yield: 8 servings

NUTRITIONAL FACTS
(PER SERVING)

CALORIES: 204

FAT: 0.9 G

PROTEIN: 4 G

CHOLESTEROL: 0 MG

SODIUM: 73 MG

FIBER: 3 G

CALCIUM: 25 MG

POTASSIUM: 146 MG

IRON: 1.2 MG

1/2 cup plus 2 tablespoons oat or barley flour

3/4 cup unbleached flour

1-1/2 teaspoons baking powder

1/2 cup sugar

1/2 cup nonfat buttermilk or plain nonfat yogurt

3 tablespoons fat-free egg substitute

1 teaspoon vanilla extract

Filling:

2 tablespoons cornstarch

2 tablespoons sugar

1/4 cup orange juice

3 cups fresh or frozen cherries, blueberries, or blackberries (or any combination)

Topping:

1/4 cup quick-cooking oats

2 tablespoons toasted wheat germ

2 tablespoons sugar

1 tablespoon frozen orange juice concentrate, thawed

1 To make the filling, combine the cornstarch, sugar, and orange juice in a saucepan. Bring to a boil over medium-low heat, stirring constantly. When the mixture begins to boil, add the berries, and continue to cook and stir until the mixture comes to a second boil. Cook and stir for another minute or 2, or until the mixture has the consistency of a pie filling.

2 To make the topping, combine the oats, wheat germ, and sugar. Add the orange juice concentrate, and stir until crumbly. Set aside.

3 Combine the flours, baking powder, and sugar, and stir to mix well. Stir in the buttermilk or yogurt, egg substitute, and vanilla extract.

4 Coat an 8-inch square pan with nonstick cooking spray. Spread the batter evenly in the pan, and spoon the fruit filling over the batter to within 1/2 inch of the edges. Sprinkle the topping over the fruit.

5 Bake at 350°F for about 35 minutes, or until the edges and topping are lightly browned.

6 Cool the cake for at least 10 minutes. Cut into squares and serve warm or at room temperature.

BERRY PEACH COFFEE CAKE

Yield: 8 servings

NUTRITIONAL FACTS
(PER SERVING)
CALORIES: 179
FAT: 0.8 G
PROTEIN: 5 G
CHOLESTEROL: 0 MG
SODIUM: 116 MG
FIBER: 2.5 G
CALCIUM: 54 MG
POTASSIUM: 197 MG
IRON: 1.6 MG

1 cup unbleached flour

1/2 cup whole wheat flour

1/4 cup plus 2 tablespoons sugar

2 teaspoons baking powder

1/4 teaspoon ground cinnamon

3/4 cup nonfat buttermilk

1 egg white

1 teaspoon vanilla extract

Topping:

2 medium peaches, peeled and cut into 1/2-inch thick slices

1/2 cup fresh or frozen blueberries or raspberries

1/4 cup toasted wheat germ

3 tablespoons brown sugar

1. Combine the flours, sugar, baking powder, and cinnamon, and stir to mix well. Stir in the buttermilk, egg white, and vanilla extract.

2. Coat a 9-inch round pan with nonstick cooking spray. Spread the batter evenly in the pan. Arrange the peach slices in a circular pattern over the batter, and spread the berries over the peaches. Combine the wheat germ and brown sugar, and sprinkle over the fruit.

3. Bake at 350°F for about 40 minutes, or until a wooden toothpick inserted in the center of the cake comes out clean.

4. Cool the cake for at least 20 minutes. Cut into wedges and serve warm or at room temperature.

PEPPERMINT BROWNIES

Yield: 16 servings

NUTRITIONAL FACTS
(PER SERVING)

CALORIES: 85

FAT: 0.5 G

PROTEIN: 1.9 G

CHOLESTEROL: 0 MG

SODIUM: 28 MG

FIBER: 0.9 G

CALCIUM: 11 MG

POTASSIUM: 42 MG

IRON: 0.5 MG

1/3 cup quick-cooking oats

1/4 cup plain nonfat yogurt

2 tablespoons water

1/2 cup unbleached flour

3/4 cup plus 2 tablespoons sugar

1/4 cup plus 2 tablespoons cocoa powder

3 egg whites

1-1/2 teaspoons vanilla extract

Icing:

1/2 cup confectioners' sugar

2 drops peppermint extract

1 drop green or red food coloring

2 teaspoons skim milk

1 Combine the oats, yogurt, and water, and set aside for 5 minutes.

2 Combine the flour, sugar, and cocoa, and stir to mix well. Add the oat mixture, egg whites, and vanilla extract to the flour mixture, and stir to mix well.

3 Coat an 8-inch square pan with nonstick cooking spray. Spread the batter evenly in the pan, and bake at 325°F for about 22 minutes, or just until the edges are firm and the center is almost set. Cool to room temperature.

4 To make the icing, combine the icing ingredients in a small bowl, and stir until smooth. If using a microwave oven, microwave the icing, uncovered, at high power for 20 seconds. If using a conventional stove top, transfer the icing to a small saucepan and place over medium heat for 20 seconds, stirring constantly. Drizzle the icing over the brownies, and let the glaze set for at least 10 minutes before cutting into squares and serving.

BANANA FUDGE CAKE

Yield: 16 servings

NUTRITIONAL FACTS
(PER SERVING)

CALORIES: 197

FAT: 0.9 G

PROTEIN: 3.5 G

CHOLESTEROL: 0 MG

SODIUM: 146 MG

FIBER: 2.5 G

CALCIUM: 25 MG

POTASSIUM: 165 MG

IRON: 1.1 MG

1 cup whole wheat flour

1 cup unbleached flour

1/2 cup cocoa powder

1-1/2 cups sugar

2 teaspoons baking soda

1/4 teaspoon salt (optional)

1-1/2 cups mashed very ripe banana
(about 3 large)

1/2 cup nonfat buttermilk

2 egg whites

1-1/2 teaspoons vanilla extract

Glaze:

1-1/2 cups confectioners' sugar

1 tablespoon plus 1-1/2 teaspoons cocoa
powder

3 tablespoons skim milk

1 teaspoon vanilla extract

1/4 cup plus 2 tablespoons chopped
walnuts (optional)

1 Combine the flours, cocoa, sugar, baking soda, and salt, if desired, and stir to mix well. Add the banana, buttermilk, egg whites, and vanilla extract, and stir to mix well.

2 Coat a 9-x-13-inch pan with nonstick cooking spray. Spread the batter evenly in the pan. Bake at 350°F for about 35 minutes, or just until a wooden toothpick inserted in the center of the cake comes out clean. Cool the cake to room temperature.

3 To make the glaze, combine the glaze ingredients in a small bowl. If using a microwave oven, microwave the glaze, uncovered, at high power for 35 seconds, or until runny. If using a conventional stove

top, transfer the glaze to a small saucepan and place over medium heat for 30 seconds, stirring constantly. Drizzle the glaze over the cake, and let harden before cutting into squares and serving.

COCOA ZUCCHINI CAKE

Yield: 16 servings

NUTRITIONAL FACTS	
(PER SERVING)	
CALORIES: 147	
FAT: 0.6 G	
PROTEIN: 3.9 G	
CHOLESTEROL: 0 MG	
SODIUM: 104 MG	
FIBER: 2.1 G	
CALCIUM: 37 MG	
POTASSIUM: 159 MG	
IRON: 1.2 MG	

1-1/2 cups unbleached flour

1 cup whole wheat flour

1 cup sugar

1/4 cup cocoa powder

2 teaspoons baking powder

1/2 teaspoon baking soda

1/4 teaspoon salt (optional)

1 teaspoon ground cinnamon

1 cup nonfat buttermilk

2 cups (packed) shredded unpeeled zucchini

3 egg whites

2 teaspoons vanilla extract

1/2 cup dark raisins or chopped walnuts

3 tablespoons confectioners' sugar (optional)

1 Combine the flours, sugar, cocoa, baking powder, baking soda, salt, and cinnamon, and stir to mix well. Stir in the buttermilk, zucchini, egg whites, and vanilla extract. Fold in the raisins or walnuts.

2 Coat a 9-x-13-inch pan with nonstick cooking spray. Spread the batter evenly in the pan, and bake at 350°F for about 35 minutes, or until a wooden toothpick inserted in the center of the cake comes out clean. Cool the cake to room temperature.

3 Sift the confectioners' sugar over the cake if desired, cut into squares, and serve.

VERY BERRY COBBLER

Yield: 8 servings

NUTRITIONAL FACTS
(PER SERVING)

CALORIES: 186

FAT: 0.5 G

PROTEIN: 3.6 G

CHOLESTEROL: 0 MG

SODIUM: 138 MG

FIBER: 2.4 G

CALCIUM: 55 MG

POTASSIUM: 272 MG

IRON: 1.1 MG

Fruit Filling:

3 tablespoons sugar

2 tablespoons cornstarch

1/4 cup plus 2 tablespoons orange juice

5 cups fresh or frozen cherries, blueberries, or blackberries (or any combination)

Topping:

2/3 cup unbleached flour

1/3 cup oat bran

1/3 cup sugar

1-1/2 teaspoons baking powder

1/2 teaspoon baking soda

3/4 cup nonfat buttermilk

1 To make the fruit filling, place the sugar and cornstarch in a medium-sized saucepan, and stir to mix well. Stir in the orange juice and fruit. Cook over medium heat, stirring constantly, for about 5 minutes, or until the mixture is thick and bubbly.

2 Coat a 2-quart casserole dish with nonstick cooking spray. Pour the fruit filling into the dish, and set aside.

3 To make the topping, combine the flour, oat bran, sugar, baking powder, and baking soda, and stir to mix well. Stir in the buttermilk. Pour the batter over the fruit.

4 Bake at 350°F for about 30 minutes, or until golden brown. Serve warm with vanilla ice milk if desired.

RASPBERRY PEACH COBBLER

Yield: 8 servings

NUTRITIONAL FACTS
(PER SERVING)

CALORIES: 209
FAT: 0.9 G
PROTEIN: 4.4 G
CHOLESTEROL: 0 MG
SODIUM: 111 MG
FIBER: 4.8 G
CALCIUM: 69 MG
POTASSIUM: 384 MG
IRON: 1.7 MG

Fruit Filling:

5 cups sliced fresh peaches
    (about 6 medium)

1-1/4 cups fresh or frozen raspberries

1/2 cup light brown sugar

4-1/2 teaspoons cornstarch

Topping:

3/4 cup oat bran

3/4 cup unbleached flour

1/4 cup sugar

2 teaspoons baking powder

3/4 cup nonfat buttermilk

1 To make the fruit filling, combine the fruit, brown sugar, and cornstarch, and toss to mix well.

2 Coat a 2-quart casserole dish with nonstick cooking spray. Pour the fruit filling into the dish, and set aside.

3 To make the topping, combine the oat bran, flour, sugar, and baking powder, and stir to mix well. Stir in the buttermilk. Drop heaping tablespoonfuls of the batter onto the fruit to make 8 biscuits.

4 Bake at 375°F for 35 to 40 minutes, or until the fruit is bubbly and the biscuits are golden brown. If the top starts to brown too quickly, cover the dish loosely with aluminum foil during the last 10 minutes of baking. Serve warm.

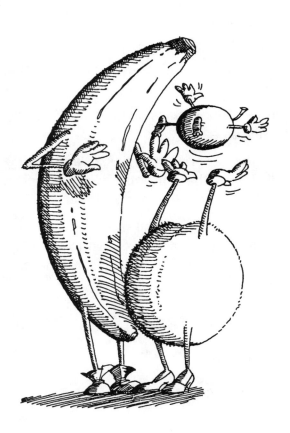

4 SWEET FAT SUBSTITUTES

L iquid sweeteners can replace all or part of the fat in cakes, muffins, quick breads, scones, cookies, and brownies, as well as in crumb toppings and some crumb and pat-in pie crusts. These syrupy liquids perform the double duty of moistening and sweetening baked goods.

A wide variety of sweeteners can be substituted for fat. Choose from honey, molasses, maple syrup, brown rice syrup, Fruit Source liquid, chocolate syrup, fruit juice concentrates, and fruit spreads or jams. You might be surprised to find that fruit juice concentrates and fruit spreads and jams have been included in this chapter, rather than in Chapter 2, "Fruitful Fat Substitutes." But these ingredients have a much higher sugar content than fruit purées and juices, and have a syrupy consistency that is similar to that of honey, maple syrup, and other liquid sweeteners.

When replacing the fat in my own recipes, I've found that different liquid sweeteners are most successful in different recipes. Honey, for instance, complements the flavor of just about any recipe, but is especially delicious in cookies. The distinctive flavors of maple syrup and molasses seem best suited to muffins, quick breads, and spice cakes. Apricot spread adds a delicious dimension to oatmeal cookies, while orange juice concentrate perks up the crumb topping of fruit crisps.

GETTING THE FAT OUT

uidelines for modifying your own recipes are presented below. (For more helpful hints on modifying recipes, see the inset on page 22.) Following these guidelines are recipes for a wide range of baked goods made irresistibly moist and delicious with sweet fat substitutes.

CAKE, MUFFIN, AND QUICK BREAD RECIPES

▓ Replace all or part of the butter, margarine, or other solid shortening in cake, muffin, and quick bread recipes with three-fourths as much liquid sweetener. If the recipe calls for oil, replace all or part of the oil with an equal amount of liquid sweetener. To prevent the baked goods from being overly sweet, reduce the sugar in the recipe by the amount of liquid sweetener added.

▓ When eliminating all of the fat from a recipe, reduce the number of eggs by half, or substitute 1 egg white for each whole egg. This will help preserve tenderness. In some recipes, you may be able to eliminate the eggs altogether by replacing each whole egg with 2 extra tablespoons of water or another liquid.

▓ To retain moistness, reduce the oven temperature by 25 degrees when baking fat-free and fat-reduced cakes, muffins, and quick breads. *Be careful not to overbake.* Bake just until a wooden toothpick inserted in the center comes out clean.

SCONE RECIPES

▓ Replace all or part of the butter, margarine, or other solid shortening in scone recipes with three-fourths as much liquid sweetener. If the recipe calls for oil, replace all or part of the oil with an equal amount of liquid sweetener. To prevent the finished product from being overly sweet, reduce the sugar in the recipe by the amount of liquid sweetener added.

▓ When eliminating all of the fat from a scone recipe, reduce the number of eggs by half, or substitute 1 egg white for each whole egg.

▓ Bake fat-free scones at 375°F.

BROWNIE RECIPES

▓ Replace all or part of the butter, margarine, or other solid shortening in brownie recipes with three-fourths as much liquid sweetener. If the recipe calls for oil, replace all or part of the oil with an equal amount of liquid sweetener. Reduce the sugar in the recipe by at least the amount of liquid sweetener added.

▓ When eliminating all of the fat from a brownie recipe, replace each egg with 2 tablespoons of water. This will help preserve the proper texture.

▓ Bake fat-free brownies at 325°F, and check for doneness a few minutes before the end of the usual baking time. Remove the brownies from the oven as soon as the edges are firm and the center is almost set.

COOKIE RECIPES

▓ Replace all or part of the butter, margarine, or other solid shortening in cookie recipes with three-fourths as much liquid sweetener. For example, if a recipe calls for 1/2 cup (8 tablespoons) of butter, replace the butter with 6 tablespoons of the desired liquid sweetener. If the recipe calls for oil, replace all of the oil with an equal amount of liquid sweetener. Reduce the sugar in the recipe by at least the amount of liquid sweetener added.

▓ When eliminating all of the fat from a cookie recipe, replace each egg with 2 tablespoons of water. This will help preserve the proper texture.

▓ Keep in mind that when you replace a solid shortening with a liquid sweetener, the cookies will have a moist, chewy texture instead of the crisp, "short" texture obtained when solid fats are used. For best results, bake fat-free cookies at 275°F to 300°F.

▓ If you prefer crisp cookies, replace only half to three-fourths of the fat with your choice of liquid sweetener. Bake these reduced-fat cookies at 300°F to 325°F.

▓ To maintain moistness, store fat-free cookies in a airtight container, placing waxed paper between the layers.

CRUMB CRUST RECIPES

- Replace all of the butter, margarine, or other solid shortening in sweet crumb crusts—graham cracker and cereal crusts, for instance—with three-fourths as much liquid sweetener. If the recipe calls for oil, replace all of the oil with an equal amount of liquid sweetener. To prevent the crust from being overly sweet, reduce the sugar in the recipe by the amount of liquid sweetener added. Mix up the crust. The mixture should look like moist, loose crumbs, and should hold together when pinched.

- Form the crust by using the back of a spoon to pat the mixture into a pie pan that has been coated with nonstick cooking spray. Periodically dip the spoon in sugar to prevent sticking.

- Bake fat-free crumb crusts at 350°F just until the edges feel firm and dry. *Be careful not to overbake.* (These crusts harden easily.) Cool and fill as desired.

CRUMB TOPPING RECIPES

- Replace the butter or margarine in crumb toppings with three-fourths as much honey, maple syrup, fruit juice concentrate, or other liquid sweetener. Reduce the sugar in the recipe by the amount of liquid sweetener added.

ORANGE MARMALADE MUFFINS

Yield: 12 muffins

NUTRITIONAL FACTS
(PER MUFFIN)

CALORIES: 113

FAT: 0.8 G

PROTEIN: 4.5 G

CHOLESTEROL: 0 MG

SODIUM: 106 MG

FIBER: 3.1 G

CALCIUM: 57 MG

POTASSIUM: 146 MG

IRON: 1 MG

1-1/4 cups whole wheat flour

1 cup oat bran or wheat bran

1 tablespoon baking powder

3/4 cup plain nonfat yogurt

1/2 cup plus 1 tablespoon orange
   marmalade

2 egg whites

1 teaspoon vanilla extract

1/3 cup chopped pecans or 3/4 cup fresh
   or frozen blueberries (optional)

1 Combine the flour, bran, and baking powder, and stir to mix well. Add the yogurt, marmalade, egg whites, and vanilla extract, and stir just until the dry ingredients are moistened. Fold in the pecans or blueberries if desired.

2 Coat muffin cups with nonstick cooking spray, and fill 3/4 full with the batter. Bake at 350°F for about 15 minutes, or just until a wooden toothpick inserted in the center of a muffin comes out clean.

3 Remove the muffin tin from the oven, and allow it to sit for 5 minutes before removing the muffins. Serve warm or at room temperature.

JAM'N'APRICOT MUFFINS

Yield: 12 muffins

NUTRITIONAL FACTS
(PER MUFFIN)

CALORIES: 130	
FAT: 0.7 G	
PROTEIN: 4 G	
CHOLESTEROL: 0 MG	
SODIUM: 108 MG	
FIBER: 3.1 G	
CALCIUM: 44 MG	
POTASSIUM: 216 MG	
IRON: 1.3 MG	

1-1/2 cups whole wheat flour

1/2 cup oat flour

1 tablespoon baking powder

1/2 cup apricot jam or preserves

2/3 cup nonfat buttermilk

2 egg whites

1 teaspoon vanilla extract

2/3 cup chopped dried apricots

1 Combine the flours and baking powder, and stir to mix well. Add the jam, buttermilk, egg whites, and vanilla extract, and stir just until the dry ingredients are moistened. Fold in the apricots.

2 Coat muffin cups with nonstick cooking spray, and fill 3/4 full with the batter. Bake at 350°F for 15 to 17 minutes, or just until a wooden toothpick inserted in the center of a muffin comes out clean.

3 Remove the muffin tin from the oven, and allow it to sit for 5 minutes before removing the muffins. Serve warm or at room temperature.

MOLASSES APPLE MUFFINS

Yield: 12 muffins

NUTRITIONAL FACTS
(PER MUFFIN)

CALORIES: 121	
FAT: 0.5 G	
PROTEIN: 3.7 G	
CHOLESTEROL: 0 MG	
SODIUM: 116 MG	
FIBER: 3.3 G	
CALCIUM: 35 MG	
POTASSIUM: 250 MG	
IRON: 1.4 MG	

2 cups whole wheat flour

1 teaspoon baking soda

1 teaspoon baking powder

1/2 teaspoon ground cinnamon

1/4 cup plus 2 tablespoons molasses

1/4 cup skim milk

2 egg whites

2 cups shredded Granny Smith apples
(about 3 medium)

1 teaspoon vanilla extract

1/3 cup dark raisins

1. Combine the flour, baking soda, baking powder, and cinnamon, and stir to mix well. Add the molasses, milk, egg whites, apples, and vanilla extract, and stir just until the dry ingredients are moistened. Fold in the raisins.

2. Coat muffin cups with nonstick cooking spray, and fill 3/4 full with the batter. Bake at 350°F for 16 to 18 minutes, or just until a wooden toothpick inserted in the center of a muffin comes out clean.

3. Remove the muffin tin from the oven, and allow it to sit for 5 minutes before removing the muffins. Serve warm or at room temperature.

SWEET CORN MUFFINS

Yield: 14 muffins

NUTRITIONAL FACTS
(PER MUFFIN)

CALORIES: 116

FAT: 0.7 G

PROTEIN: 3.6 G

CHOLESTEROL: 0 MG

SODIUM: 137 MG

FIBER: 2.8 G

CALCIUM: 60 MG

POTASSIUM: 231 MG

IRON: 1.2 MG

1-1/4 cups whole wheat flour

1 cup whole grain cornmeal

1 tablespoon baking powder

1/2 teaspoon baking soda

1-1/3 cups nonfat buttermilk

1/4 cup plus 2 tablespoons molasses
or sugarcane syrup

2 egg whites

1/2 cup chopped dates

1. Combine the flour, cornmeal, baking powder, and baking soda, and stir to mix well. Add the buttermilk, molasses or sugarcane syrup, and egg whites, and stir just until the dry ingredients are moistened. Fold in the dates.

2. Coat muffin cups with nonstick cooking spray, and fill 2/3 full with the batter. Bake at 350°F for about 15 minutes, or just until a wooden toothpick inserted in the center of a muffin comes out clean.

3. Remove the muffin tin from the oven, and allow it to sit for 5 minutes before removing the muffins. Serve warm or at room temperature.

REFRIGERATOR BRAN MUFFINS

Yield: 12 muffins

NUTRITIONAL FACTS
(PER MUFFIN)
CALORIES: 114
FAT: 0.6 G
PROTEIN: 4.3 G
CHOLESTEROL: 0 MG
SODIUM: 97 MG
FIBER: 3.9 G
CALCIUM: 49 MG
POTASSIUM: 334 MG
IRON: 1.9 MG

1-1/4 cups whole wheat flour

1 teaspoon baking soda

1-1/2 cups wheat bran

3/4 cup nonfat buttermilk

1/2 cup orange or apple juice

1/4 cup plus 2 tablespoons molasses or honey

2 egg whites

1/2 cup dark raisins or chopped dried fruit

1/4 cup hulled sunflower seeds (optional)

1 Combine the flour and baking soda, and stir to mix well. Add the remaining ingredients, and stir just until the dry ingredients are moistened. Cover, and refrigerate overnight or up to 3 days.

2 When ready to bake, stir the batter well. Coat muffin cups with nonstick cooking spray, and fill 3/4 full with the batter. Bake at 350°F for 16 to 18 minutes, or just until a wooden toothpick inserted in the center of a muffin comes out clean.

3 Remove the muffin tin from the oven, and allow it to sit for 5 minutes before removing the muffins. Serve warm or at room temperature.

STRAWBERRY STREUSEL MUFFINS

Yield: 12 muffins

1-1/2 cups whole wheat flour

1/2 cup oat flour

1/3 cup sugar

1 tablespoon baking powder

1 cup puréed strawberries
    (about 2 cups fresh)

1/4 cup plus 2 tablespoons orange juice

2 egg whites

Topping:

1/4 cup quick-cooking oats

1 tablespoon whole wheat flour

2 tablespoons sugar

1 tablespoon frozen orange juice
    concentrate, thawed

1. To make the topping, stir the topping ingredients together until moist and crumbly. Set aside.

2. Combine the flours, sugar, and baking powder, and stir to mix well. Add the strawberries, orange juice, and egg whites, and stir just until the dry ingredients are moistened.

3. Coat muffin cups with nonstick cooking spray, and fill 3/4 full with the batter. Sprinkle the topping over the batter. Bake at 350°F for about 15 minutes, or just until a wooden toothpick inserted in the center of a muffin comes out clean.

4. Remove the muffin tin from the oven, and allow it to sit for 5 minutes before removing the muffins. Serve warm or at room temperature.

BANANA GINGERBREAD

Yield: 16 slices

NUTRITIONAL FACTS
(PER SLICE)

CALORIES:	89
FAT:	0.6 G
PROTEIN:	2.8 G
CHOLESTEROL:	0 MG
SODIUM:	74 MG
FIBER:	2.5 G
CALCIUM:	19 MG
POTASSIUM:	209 MG
IRON:	1 MG

2 cups whole wheat flour

1/4 cup toasted wheat germ

1 teaspoon baking powder

1 teaspoon baking soda

1-1/2 teaspoons ground ginger

1 teaspoon ground cinnamon

1-1/2 cups mashed very ripe banana (about 3 large)

1/4 cup molasses

1 Combine the flour, wheat germ, baking powder, baking soda, and spices, and stir to mix well. Add the remaining ingredients, and stir just until the dry ingredients are moistened.

2 Coat an 8-x-4-inch loaf pan with nonstick cooking spray. Spread the mixture evenly in the pan, and bake at 325°F for 40 to 45 minutes, or just until a wooden toothpick inserted in the center of the loaf comes out clean.

3 Remove the bread from the oven, and let sit for 10 minutes. Invert the loaf onto a wire rack, turn right side up, and cool before slicing and serving.

FRESH PEAR SCONES

Yield: 12 scones

NUTRITIONAL FACTS
(PER SCONE)

CALORIES: 97

FAT: 0.3 G

PROTEIN: 2.7 G

CHOLESTEROL: 0 MG

SODIUM: 90 MG

FIBER: 1.8 G

CALCIUM: 33 MG

POTASSIUM: 107 MG

IRON: 1.1 MG

1 cup unbleached flour

3/4 cup whole wheat flour

1 tablespoon baking powder

3 tablespoons maple syrup

3 tablespoons fat-free egg substitute

3/4 cup finely chopped fresh pears
(about 1 medium)

1/3 cup currants or dark raisins

2–3 tablespoons skim milk

Skim milk

1 Combine the flours and baking powder, and stir to mix well. Stir in the remaining ingredients, adding just enough of the milk to form a stiff dough.

2 Form the dough into a ball, and turn onto a lightly floured surface. With floured hands, pat the dough into a 7-inch circle.

3 Coat a baking sheet with nonstick cooking spray. Place the dough on the sheet, and use a sharp floured knife to cut it into 12 wedges. Pull the wedges out slightly to leave a 1/2-inch space between them. Brush the tops lightly with skim milk.

4 Bake at 375°F for about 20 minutes, or until lightly browned. Transfer to a serving plate, and serve hot.

HONEY OAT SCONES

Yield: 12 scones

NUTRITIONAL FACTS (PER SCONE)
CALORIES: 123
FAT: 0.6 G
PROTEIN: 3.4 G
CHOLESTEROL: 0 MG
SODIUM: 97 MG
FIBER: 1.4 G
CALCIUM: 33 MG
POTASSIUM: 94 MG
IRON: 1.2 MG

1-1/2 cups unbleached flour

1 cup quick-cooking oats

1 tablespoon baking powder

1/4 cup honey

3 tablespoons fat-free egg substitute

1/3 cup dark raisins

1/4 cup plus 2 tablespoons nonfat buttermilk

Skim milk

1 Combine the flour, oats, and baking powder, and stir to mix well. Stir in the honey, egg substitute, raisins, and buttermilk, adding just enough of the buttermilk to form a stiff dough.

2 Form the dough into a ball, and turn onto a lightly floured surface. With floured hands, pat the dough into a 7-inch circle.

3 Coat a baking sheet with nonstick cooking spray. Place the dough on the sheet, and use a sharp floured knife to cut it into 12 wedges. Pull the wedges out slightly to leave a 1/2-inch space between them. Brush the tops lightly with skim milk.

4 Bake at 375°F for about 20 minutes, or until lightly browned. Transfer to a serving plate, and serve hot.

MAPLE SPICE CAKE

Yield: 16 servings

NUTRITIONAL FACTS
(PER SERVING)

CALORIES: 216

FAT: 0.3 G

PROTEIN: 4 G

CHOLESTEROL: 0 MG

SODIUM: 96 MG

FIBER: 1.5 G

CALCIUM: 76 MG

POTASSIUM: 162 MG

IRON: 1.2 MG

1-1/3 cups unbleached flour
1-1/3 cups whole wheat flour
1 cup sugar
1 tablespoon baking powder
1 teaspoon ground cinnamon
1/2 teaspoon ground ginger
1/4 teaspoon ground nutmeg
1-1/3 cups skim milk
2/3 cup maple syrup
4 egg whites

Fluffy Maple Frosting:

1 cup maple syrup
2 egg whites

1 Combine the flours, sugar, baking powder, and spices, and stir to mix well. Add the milk, maple syrup, and egg whites, and stir to mix well.

2 Coat a 9-x-13-inch pan with nonstick cooking spray. Spread the batter evenly in the pan, and bake at 350°F for 30 to 35 minutes, or just until a wooden toothpick inserted in the center of the cake comes out clean. Cool the cake to room temperature.

3 To make the frosting, place the maple syrup in a small saucepan. Bring the syrup to a boil over medium heat, and continue cooking without stirring until the temperature reaches 240°F on a candy thermometer inserted in the liquid. (If you don't have a candy thermometer, place a drop of syrup in a cup of cold water. When the syrup has reached the proper temperature, it will form a soft ball in the water and then flatten upon removal.) Just before the syrup reaches the desired temperature, beat the egg whites to soft peaks with an electric mixer. Slowly add the syrup to the egg whites while

beating at high speed. Continue beating for about 5 minutes, or until the icing is glossy and firm enough to spread.

4 Spread the frosting over the cooled cake. Cut into squares and serve immediately, or refrigerate to prevent the frosting from separating.

GRANNY'S APPLE CAKE

Yield: 16 servings

NUTRITIONAL FACTS (PER SERVING)
CALORIES: 188
FAT: 0.4 G
PROTEIN: 3.4 G
CHOLESTEROL: 0 MG
SODIUM: 119 MG
FIBER: 2.3 G
CALCIUM: 14 MG
POTASSIUM: 141 MG
IRON: 1.2 MG

1-1/4 cups whole wheat flour
1-1/4 cups unbleached flour
3/4 cup sugar
2 teaspoons baking soda
2-1/2 teaspoons ground cinnamon
3/4 cup maple syrup
4 egg whites
2 teaspoons vanilla extract
4 cups chopped Granny Smith apples (about 5 medium)
1/2 cup dark raisins
1/2 cup chopped walnuts (optional)

1 Combine the flours, sugar, baking soda, and cinnamon, and stir to mix well. Add the maple syrup, egg whites, and vanilla extract, and stir to mix well. Fold in the remaining ingredients.

2 Coat a 9-x-13-inch pan with nonstick cooking spray. Spread batter evenly in pan, and bake at 350°F for 40 to 50 minutes, or just until a wooden toothpick inserted in center of cake comes out clean.

3 Cool the cake for at least 20 minutes. Cut into squares and serve warm or at room temperature.

THE ICING ON THE CAKE

Traditionally, recipes for icing 9-x-13-inch cakes have often called for up to 3 cups of confectioners' sugar and a stick of butter. But is there an alternative that not only is healthy, but also satisfies everyone's expectations of a sweet and creamy topping? Of course there is! Instead of being laden with fat, the icings and frostings in this book are made with nonfat ricotta cheese, nonfat cream cheese, and nonfat yogurt, and contain 30 to 50 percent less sugar than traditional ones do. The following suggestions summarize many of the frostings and other no-bake toppings used within these pages, and present some additional ideas as well.

▓ Dust the tops of chocolate cakes with a bit of confectioners' sugar. Try sifting powdered maple sugar over the tops of spice cakes and over banana cakes and other fruit-flavored treats.

▓ Place 2 cups of light ricotta cheese, 1 teaspoon of vanilla extract, and 3 to 4 tablespoons of honey or maple syrup in a blender or food processor, and process until smooth. This recipe makes enough for a 9-x-13-inch cake. Try it on spice cakes and on banana and other fruit-flavored cakes.

▓ Instead of making a frosting, spread a thin layer of fruit spread or preserves over the tops of cakes. Use raspberry spread on chocolate cakes, pineapple spread on banana cakes, and apricot or peach spread on spice cakes.

▓ Spread cakes with yogurt cheese—a sweet, creamy spread made by draining the whey from yogurt. Simply place any flavor yogurt in a large funnel lined with cheesecloth or a coffee filter. Place the funnel in the mouth of a quart jar, and place the jar in the refrigerator for 8 hours, or until the amount is reduced by half. Do not use yogurts that contain gelatin, as they will not separate. Two cups of yogurt cheese is enough to cover a 9-x-13-inch cake. Try vanilla, coffee, or raspberry yogurt on chocolate cakes; vanilla, banana, or pineapple yogurt on banana cakes; and lemon or vanilla yogurt on lemon and carrot cakes.

▓ For a fat-free cream cheese icing, place 1 cup nonfat cream cheese, 1 cup nonfat ricotta, 1/2 cup sugar, and 1 teaspoon vanilla extract in a food processor, and process until smooth. Spread over carrot cakes, pineapple cakes, and spice cakes.

▓ For a fluffy, no-fuss whipped cream-type frosting, fold 1/2 to 1 cup of any flavor nonfat yogurt into 1 to 1-1/2 cups of light whipped topping. Spread the frosting over a 9-x-13-inch cake. (If the frosting is a bit thin, refrigerate the frosted cake for an hour or two and it will thicken.) Use vanilla yogurt on cakes of any flavor, lemon yogurt on lemon cakes, banana yogurt on banana cakes, and coffee or raspberry yogurt on chocolate cakes. Adding yogurt to whipped toppings creates a creamier flavor and texture, and adds some nutrition to an otherwise nutrient-poor product.

BLACK FOREST CAKE

Yield: 10 servings

NUTRITIONAL FACTS
(PER SERVING)
CALORIES: 219
FAT: 0.9 G
PROTEIN: 3.4 G
CHOLESTEROL: 0 MG
SODIUM: 116 MG
FIBER: 3.2 G
CALCIUM: 9 MG
POTASSIUM: 73 MG
IRON: 1.4 MG

This cake is made in a flan or tiara pan. The bottom of the pan has a raised center that makes an ideal place to put a filling after the cake has been baked, cooled, and inverted.

1 cup unbleached flour

1/2 cup oat flour

3/4 cup sugar

1/4 cup cocoa powder

1 teaspoon baking soda

1 teaspoon vanilla extract

1/4 cup chocolate syrup

1-1/2 teaspoons white vinegar

1 cup water

Filling:

1 can (20 ounces) light (low-sugar) cherry
  pie filling

Meringue Topping:

2 egg whites, brought to room temperature

1/8 teaspoon cream of tartar

5 tablespoons sugar

1 teaspoon vanilla or almond extract

1 Combine the flours, sugar, cocoa, and baking soda, and stir to mix well. In a separate bowl, combine the vanilla extract, chocolate syrup, vinegar, and water. Add the chocolate mixture to the flour mixture, and stir to mix well.

2 Coat a 10-inch flan pan with nonstick cooking spray. Spread the batter evenly in the pan, and bake at 350°F for 15 to 20 minutes, or just until a wooden toothpick inserted in the center of the cake comes out clean.

3 Cool the cake to room temperature. Then invert onto a baking sheet. Fill the depression in the top of the cake with the cherry pie filling.

4 To make the meringue topping, whip the egg whites and cream of tartar with an electric mixer until soft peaks form. Still beating, slowly add the sugar and vanilla or almond extract. Continue to beat until stiff peaks form.

5 Pipe or spoon the meringue in a ring around the outer edge of the cherry filling. Place the cake in a 400°F oven for 3 to 5 minutes, or until the meringue is lightly browned.

6 Cool the cake to room temperature. Slice and serve immediately, or refrigerate to prevent the meringue from separating.

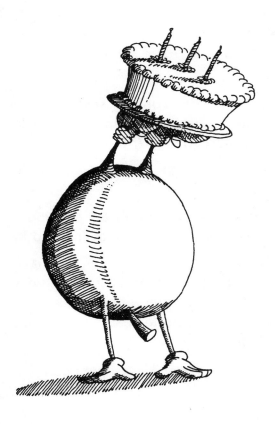

BLUEBERRY UPSIDE-DOWN CAKE

Yield: 9 servings

NUTRITIONAL FACTS
(PER SERVING)

CALORIES: 211	
FAT: 0.6 G	
PROTEIN: 4 G	
CHOLESTEROL: 0 MG	
SODIUM: 111 MG	
FIBER: 1.4 G	
CALCIUM: 44 MG	
POTASSIUM: 130 MG	
IRON: 1.3 MG	

2 tablespoons frozen apple or orange juice concentrate, thawed

1/4 cup brown sugar

1-1/4 cups fresh or frozen blueberries

1-1/4 cups unbleached flour

1/3 cup oat flour

1-1/2 teaspoons baking powder

1/2 cup sugar

2/3 cup skim milk

1/3 cup honey

2 egg whites

1 teaspoon vanilla extract

1. Coat an 8-inch square pan with nonstick cooking spray. Evenly spread the juice concentrate on the bottom of the pan, and sprinkle with the brown sugar. Arrange the blueberries over the brown sugar.

2. Combine the flours, baking powder, and sugar, and stir to mix well. Add the remaining ingredients, and stir to mix well.

3. Pour the batter over the blueberries, spreading evenly. Bake at 350°F for 35 to 45 minutes, or just until a wooden toothpick inserted in the center of the cake comes out clean.

4. Cool the cake at room temperature for 10 minutes. Loosen the sides of the cake by running a sharp knife along the edges, and invert onto a serving platter. Serve warm or at room temperature, topping each piece with vanilla ice milk if desired.

APPLE RAISIN CRISP

Yield: 6 servings

NUTRITIONAL FACTS
(PER SERVING)

CALORIES: 139

FAT: 0.9 G

PROTEIN: 2 G

CHOLESTEROL: 0 MG

SODIUM: 5 MG

FIBER: 2.9 G

CALCIUM: 17 MG

POTASSIUM: 228 MG

IRON: 0.9 MG

Fruit Filling:

5 cups thinly sliced peeled fresh apples (about 6 medium)

1-1/2 teaspoons cornstarch

1/3 cup dark raisins

3 tablespoons frozen apple juice concentrate, thawed

Topping:

3 tablespoons toasted wheat germ

1/2 cup quick-cooking oats

3 tablespoons light brown sugar

1/2 teaspoon ground cinnamon

1 tablespoon frozen apple juice concentrate, thawed

1. To make the fruit filling, toss the apple slices with the cornstarch. Add the raisins and juice concentrate, and toss to mix. Place the mixture in a 9-inch deep-dish pie pan.

2. To make the topping, combine the topping ingredients and mix until moist and crumbly. Sprinkle the topping over the fruit.

3. Bake uncovered at 375°F for 25 minutes. Cover the dish loosely with foil to prevent overbrowning, and continue baking for 15 to 20 minutes, or until the filling is bubbly and the topping is golden brown. Serve warm.

SWEET CHERRY CRISP

Yield: 8 servings

NUTRITIONAL FACTS (PER SERVING)
CALORIES: 165
FAT: 0.8 G
PROTEIN: 3.2 G
CHOLESTEROL: 0 MG
SODIUM: 4 MG
FIBER: 2.8 G
CALCIUM: 31 MG
POTASSIUM: 348 MG
IRON: 1.3 MG

Fruit Filling:

6 cups pitted sweet cherries or 2 packages (12 ounces each) frozen cherries, thawed

4-1/2 teaspoons cornstarch

2 tablespoons sugar

Topping:

1/2 cup plus 2 tablespoons quick-cooking oats

1/4 cup light brown sugar

1/4 cup toasted wheat germ

4-1/2 teaspoons frozen orange or apple juice concentrate, thawed

1. To make the fruit filling, combine the cherries with the cornstarch and the sugar, and toss to mix well.

2. Coat a 2-quart casserole dish with nonstick cooking spray. Pour the fruit filling into the dish, and set aside.

3. To make the topping, combine the topping ingredients and mix until moist and crumbly. Sprinkle the topping over the fruit.

4. Bake at 375°F for 30 to 35 minutes, or until the filling is bubbly and the topping is golden brown. Serve warm.

FRUITFUL GRAHAM CRACKER PIE CRUST

Yield: One 9-inch pie
crust for 8 servings

NUTRITIONAL FACTS (PER SERVING)
CALORIES: 93
FAT: 0.1 G
PROTEIN: 1.6 G
CHOLESTEROL: 0 MG
SODIUM: 127 MG
FIBER: 0.5 G
CALCIUM: 9 MG
POTASSIUM: 79 MG
IRON: 0.7 MG

If fat-free graham crackers aren't available, just use regular graham crackers, as they are quite low in fat. Use your imagination and choose the flavor fruit spread that would best complement your filling.

8 large (2-1/2-x-5-inch) fat-free graham crackers

3 tablespoons fruit spread or jam, any flavor

1 Break the crackers into pieces, and place in the bowl of a food processor or in a blender. Process into fine crumbs. Measure the crumbs. There should be 1-1/4 cups.

2 Return the crumbs to the food processor, and add the fruit spread. Process until moist and crumbly.

3 Coat a 9-inch pie pan with nonstick cooking spray. Use the back of a spoon to press the crumbs against the sides and bottom of the pan, forming an even crust. Periodically dip the spoon in sugar to prevent sticking.

4 Bake the pie shell at 350°F for 10 minutes, or until the edges feel firm and dry. Cool the crust to room temperature, and fill as desired.

CRUNCHY CEREAL PIE CRUST

Yield: One 9-inch pie crust for 8 servings

NUTRITIONAL FACTS
(PER SERVING)

CALORIES: 86

FAT: 0.2 MG

PROTEIN: 3.3 G

CHOLESTEROL: 0 MG

SODIUM: 159 MG

FIBER: 0.6 G

CALCIUM: 9 MG

POTASSIUM: 133 MG

IRON: 1.6 MG

This crust, like the one on page 123, may be tailor-made for different fillings by the use of different fruit spreads.

5 ounces (about 2-1/2 cups) oat flakes, or oat flakes with almonds ready-to-eat cereal

3 tablespoons fruit spread or jam, any flavor

1 Place the cereal in the bowl of a food processor or in a blender. Process into fine crumbs. Measure the crumbs. There should be about 1-1/4 cups.

2 Return the crumbs to the food processor, and add the fruit spread. Process until moist and crumbly.

3 Coat a 9-inch pie pan with nonstick cooking spray. Use the back of a spoon to press the crumbs against the sides and bottom of the pan, forming an even crust. Periodically dip the spoon in sugar to prevent sticking.

4 Bake the pie shell at 350°F for 10 to 12 minutes, or until the edges feel firm and dry. Cool the crust to room temperature, and fill as desired.

STRAWBERRY BANANA PIE

Yield: 8 servings

1 prepared Fruitful Graham Cracker Pie Crust, made with strawberry fruit spread (page 123)

Glaze:

1/3 cup sugar

3 tablespoons cornstarch

1-1/2 cups cran-strawberry juice, or another strawberry juice blend

Filling:

2 cups fresh strawberries, cut in half

2 cups sliced fresh bananas

1 To make the glaze, combine the sugar and cornstarch in a medium-sized saucepan. Slowly stir in the juice. Place over medium heat and bring to a boil, stirring constantly. Reduce the heat to low, and cook and stir for another minute. Remove the saucepan from the heat, and set aside for 15 minutes.

2 Stir the glaze, and spoon a thin layer over the bottom of the pie crust. Arrange half of the strawberries and half of the bananas over the bottom of the crust. Spoon half of the remaining glaze over the fruit. Arrange the rest of the fruit over the glaze, and top with the remaining glaze.

3 Chill for several hours, or until the glaze is set. Cut into wedges and serve cold.

PEACH PIZZAZ PIE

Yield: 8 servings

1 prepared Crunchy Cereal Pie Crust, made with peach fruit spread (page 124)

Glaze:

1/3 cup sugar

3 tablespoons cornstarch

1-1/2 cups peach nectar

Filling:

3 cups sliced fresh peaches (about 4 medium)

1 cup fresh blueberries or raspberries

1 To make the glaze, combine the sugar and cornstarch in a medium-sized saucepan. Slowly stir in the nectar. Place over medium heat and bring to a boil, stirring constantly. Reduce the heat to low, and cook for another minute. Remove the saucepan from the heat, and set aside for 15 minutes.

2 Stir the glaze, and spoon a thin layer over the bottom of the pie crust. Arrange half of the peaches in a circular pattern over the bottom of the crust. Top with the blueberries, and spoon half of the remaining glaze over the berries. Arrange the rest of the peaches over the glaze, and top with the remaining glaze.

3 Chill for several hours, or until the glaze is set. Cut into wedges and serve cold.

HONEY GRANOLA BARS

Yield: 12 servings

NUTRITIONAL FACTS
(PER SERVING)

CALORIES: 95

FAT: 0.7 G

PROTEIN: 2.4 G

CHOLESTEROL: 0 MG

SODIUM: 2 MG

FIBER: 1.8 G

CALCIUM: 9 MG

POTASSIUM: 95 MG

IRON: 0.8 MG

1-1/4 cups quick-cooking oats

1/4 cup whole wheat flour

1/4 cup toasted wheat germ

1/4 teaspoon ground cinnamon

1/4 cup plus 2 tablespoons honey

1/3 cup dark raisins or chopped dried apricots

1 Combine the oats, flour, wheat germ, and cinnamon, and stir to mix well. Add the honey, and stir until the mixture is moist and crumbly. Fold in the raisins or apricots.

2 Coat an 8-inch square pan with nonstick cooking spray. Pat the mixture into the pan, and bake at 300°F for 18 to 20 minutes, or until lightly browned.

3 Cool to room temperature, cut into bars, and serve.

HONEY OAT BROWNIES

Yield: 16 servings

3/4 cup quick-cooking oats

1/4 cup unbleached flour

1/4 cup plus 2 tablespoons cocoa powder

1/2 cup sugar

1/8 teaspoon baking powder

1/8 teaspoon salt (optional)

1/4 cup plus 2 tablespoons honey

1/4 cup water

1 teaspoon vanilla extract

1/4 cup chopped walnuts (optional)

1. Combine the oats, flour, cocoa, sugar, baking powder, and salt, if desired, and stir to mix well. Stir in the remaining ingredients.

2. Coat an 8-inch square pan with nonstick cooking spray. Spread the batter evenly in the pan, and bake at 325°F for about 20 minutes, or until the edges are firm and the center is almost set.

3. Cool to room temperature, cut into squares, and serve.

BROWN RICE BISCOTTI

Yield: 24 biscotti

NUTRITIONAL FACTS
(PER BISCOTTI)

CALORIES: 60

FAT: 0.5 G

PROTEIN: 1.5 G

CHOLESTEROL: 0 MG

SODIUM: 35 MG

FIBER: 0.7 G

CALCIUM: 8 MG

POTASSIUM: 52 MG

IRON: 0.5 MG

1 cup unbleached flour

1/2 cup whole wheat flour

1/2 cup brown rice flour

1/4 cup sugar

2 teaspoons baking powder

1/4 cup honey or brown rice syrup

3 egg whites

1 teaspoon vanilla extract

1/3 cup finely chopped dried apricots

2 tablespoons finely ground pecans

1 Combine the flours, sugar, and baking powder, and stir to mix well. Add the remaining ingredients, and stir just until the dough holds together.

2 Turn the dough onto a lightly floured surface, and shape into two 9-x-2-inch logs. Coat a baking sheet with nonstick cooking spray, and place the logs on the sheet. Bake at 350°F for 18 to 20 minutes, or until lightly browned.

3 Cool the logs at room temperature for 10 minutes. Then use a serrated knife to slice the logs diagonally into 1/2-inch-thick slices.

4 Place the slices on a baking sheet in a single layer, and bake at 325°F for 18 to 20 minutes, or until lightly browned, turning after 10 minutes.

5 Transfer the biscotti to wire racks, and cool completely. Serve immediately or store in an airtight container.

CHOCOLATE OATMEAL JUMBLES

Yield: 42 cookies

NUTRITIONAL FACTS (PER COOKIE)
CALORIES: 46
FAT: 0.9 G
PROTEIN: 1.1 G
CHOLESTEROL: 0 MG
SODIUM: 27 MG
FIBER: 0.9 G
CALCIUM: 4 MG
POTASSIUM: 46 MG
IRON: 0.4 MG

1 cup whole wheat flour

1 cup quick-cooking oats

1/4 cup sugar

2 tablespoons cocoa powder

1 teaspoon baking soda

1/2 cup plus 2 tablespoons chocolate syrup

2 tablespoons plus 2 teaspoons water

1 teaspoon vanilla extract

1/4 cup dark raisins

1/4 cup chopped walnuts

1/4 cup chocolate chips

1 Combine the flour, oats, sugar, cocoa, and baking soda, and stir to mix well. Add the chocolate syrup, water, and vanilla extract, and stir to mix well. Stir in the remaining ingredients.

2 Coat a baking sheet with nonstick cooking spray. Drop rounded tea-spoonfuls of dough onto the baking sheet, placing them 1-1/2 inches apart. Slightly flatten each cookie with the tip of a spoon.

3 Bake at 275°F for 18 to 20 minutes, or until lightly browned. Cool the cookies on the pan for 1 minute. Then transfer the cookies to wire racks, and cool completely. Serve immediately, or transfer to an airtight container and arrange in single layers separated by sheets of waxed paper.

MOLASSES OATMEAL TREATS

Yield: 42 cookies

NUTRITIONAL FACTS
(PER COOKIE)

CALORIES: 43	
FAT: 0.3 G	
PROTEIN: 1 G	
CHOLESTEROL: 0 MG	
SODIUM: 27 MG	
FIBER: 1 G	
CALCIUM: 12 MG	
POTASSIUM: 105 MG	
IRON: 0.8 MG	

1 cup whole wheat flour

1 cup quick-cooking oats

1/4 cup sugar

1 teaspoon baking soda

1/2 cup plus 2 tablespoons molasses

2 tablespoons plus 2 teaspoons water

1 teaspoon vanilla extract

1/4 cup toasted wheat germ

1 cup bran flake-and-raisin cereal

2/3 cup chopped dried apricots or other dried fruit

1 Combine the flour, oats, sugar, and baking soda, and stir to mix well. Add the molasses, water, and vanilla extract, and stir to mix well. Stir in the remaining ingredients.

2 Coat a baking sheet with nonstick cooking spray. Drop rounded tea-spoonfuls of dough onto the baking sheet, placing them 1-1/2 inches apart. Slightly flatten each cookie with the tip of a spoon.

3 Bake at 275°F for 18 to 20 minutes, or until lightly browned. Cool the cookies on the pan for 1 minute. Then transfer the cookies to wire racks, and cool completely. Serve immediately, or transfer to an airtight container and arrange in single layers separated by sheets of waxed paper.

WHOLE WHEAT GINGER SNAPS

Yield: 24 cookies

NUTRITIONAL FACTS
(PER COOKIE)

CALORIES: 41

FAT: 0.1 G

PROTEIN: 0.9 G

CHOLESTEROL: 0 MG

SODIUM: 26 MG

FIBER: 0.8 G

CALCIUM: 8 MG

POTASSIUM: 72 MG

IRON: 0.4 MG

1-1/3 cups whole wheat flour

1/4 cup sugar

3/4 teaspoon baking soda

1/2 teaspoon ground ginger

1/4 cup molasses

3 tablespoons frozen orange juice
    concentrate, thawed

1 Combine the flour, sugar, baking soda, and ginger, and stir to mix well. Stir in the molasses and orange juice concentrate.

2 Coat a baking sheet with nonstick cooking spray. Roll the dough into 1-inch balls, and place 1-1/2 inches apart on the baking sheet. (If the dough is too sticky to handle, place it in the freezer for a few minutes.) Using the bottom of a glass dipped in sugar, flatten the cookies to 1/4-inch thickness.

3 Bake at 300°F for about 12 minutes, or until lightly browned. Cool the cookies on the pan for 1 minute. Then transfer the cookies to wire racks, and cool completely. Serve immediately, or transfer to an airtight container and arrange in single layers separated by sheets of waxed paper.

BANANA MUESLI COOKIES

Yield: 30 cookies

NUTRITIONAL FACTS
(PER COOKIE)

CALORIES: 46

FAT: 0.4 G

PROTEIN: 1.2 G

CHOLESTEROL: 0 MG

SODIUM: 28 MG

FIBER: 1 G

CALCIUM: 9 MG

POTASSIUM: 60 MG

IRON: 0.3 MG

1 cup whole wheat flour

1 cup quick-cooking oats

3/4 teaspoon baking soda

2/3 cup mashed very ripe banana
  (about 1-1/2 large)

1/4 cup plus 2 tablespoons maple syrup

1 cup ready-to-eat muesli cereal

30 pecan halves (optional)

1 Combine the flour, oats, and baking soda, and stir to mix well. Add the banana and maple syrup, and stir to mix well. Stir in the cereal.

2 Coat a baking sheet with nonstick cooking spray. Roll the dough into 1-inch balls, and place 1-1/2 inches apart on the baking sheet. (If the dough is too sticky to handle, place it in the freezer for a few minutes.) Using the bottom of a glass dipped in sugar, flatten the cookies to 1/4-inch thickness. As an alternative, press a pecan half in the center of each cookie to flatten the dough.

3 Bake at 275°F for about 18 minutes, or until lightly browned. Cool the cookies on the pan for 1 minute. Then transfer the cookies to wire racks, and cool completely. Serve immediately, or transfer to an airtight container and arrange in single layers separated by sheets of waxed paper.

JAM'N'OATMEAL COOKIES

Yield: 60 cookies

NUTRITIONAL FACTS
(PER COOKIE)

CALORIES: 48	
FAT: 0.2 G	
PROTEIN: 0.9 G	
CHOLESTEROL: 0 MG	
SODIUM: 15 MG	
FIBER: 0.8 G	
CALCIUM: 7 MG	
POTASSIUM: 55 MG	
IRON: 0.4 MG	

1-1/2 cups whole wheat flour

2 cups quick-cooking oats

3/4 cup light brown sugar

1-1/4 teaspoons baking soda

1/2 teaspoon ground cinnamon

3/4 cup jam or fruit spread (try apricot, peach, pineapple, raspberry, or strawberry)

1/4 cup water

1 teaspoon vanilla extract

3/4 cup dark raisins, chopped dried fruit, or chopped nuts

1 Combine the flour, oats, brown sugar, baking soda, and cinnamon, and stir to mix well. Add the jam or fruit spread, water, and vanilla extract, and stir to mix well. Stir in the fruit or nuts.

2 Coat a baking sheet with nonstick cooking spray. Drop rounded teaspoonfuls of dough onto the baking sheet, placing them 1-1/2 inches apart. Slightly flatten each cookie with the tip of a spoon.

3 Bake at 275°F for about 18 minutes, or until lightly browned. Cool the cookies on the pan for 1 minute. Then transfer the cookies to wire racks, and cool completely. Serve immediately, or transfer to an airtight container and arrange in single layers separated by sheets of waxed paper.

APRICOT TEA COOKIES

Yield: 35 cookies

NUTRITIONAL FACTS (PER COOKIE)	
CALORIES: 45	
FAT: 0.2 G	
PROTEIN: 1 G	
CHOLESTEROL: 0 MG	
SODIUM: 19 MG	
FIBER: 0.7 G	
CALCIUM: 4 MG	
POTASSIUM: 43 MG	
IRON: 0.5 MG	

1-1/4 cups unbleached flour

1 cup oat bran

1/4 cup plus 2 tablespoons sugar

3/4 teaspoon baking soda

1/4 cup plus 2 tablespoons apricot jam

1/4 cup water

1/2 cup chopped dried apricots

36 pecan halves or whole almonds (optional)

1 Combine the flour, oat bran, sugar, and baking soda, and stir to mix well. Add the jam and water, and stir to mix well. Stir in the dried apricots.

2 Coat a baking sheet with nonstick cooking spray. Roll the dough into 1-inch balls, and place 1-1/2 inches apart on the baking sheet. (If the dough is too sticky to handle, place it in the freezer for a few minutes.) Using the bottom of a glass dipped in sugar, flatten the cookies to 1/4-inch thickness. As an alternative, press a pecan half or almond in the center of each cookie to flatten the dough.

3 Bake at 300°F for 15 to 18 minutes, or until lightly browned. Cool the cookies on the pan for 1 minute. Then transfer the cookies to wire racks, and cool completely. Serve immediately, or transfer to an airtight container and arrange in single layers separated by sheets of waxed paper.

Black Forest Cake (page 118)

Top Left: Chewy Coconut Brownies and
Honey Oat Brownies (pages 167 and 128)
Top Right: Fresh Pear Scones (page 112)
Bottom: Oatmeal Raisin Cookies (page 168)

5 PRUNING FAT

Rich in fiber and carbohydrates, prunes have a superb moisture-holding capacity, which makes them an excellent fat substitute in muffins, quick breads, cakes, cookies, and brownies. When you incorporate prunes into baked goods, you not only eliminate fat, you also add fiber and nutrients.

Will prunes overpower the flavor of your finished product? Not when used according to the guidelines provided in this chapter. The subtle prune flavor actually enhances the taste of many baked goods. What about the laxative effect of prunes? Prunes are a minor component in most of these recipes, and should not cause any undesirable effects for most people.

When replacing fats with prunes, you will use one of two basic recipes: Prune Purée and Prune Butter. Prune Purée has a mild fruity flavor that works well as a fat substitute in all baked goods, and is especially good when used in cookies. (The texture of cookies made with Prune Purée is very similar to that of cookies made with fat.) The fat in baked goods is replaced by half as much of the purée. When you use one-fourth cup of the purée, which contains 40 calories, to replace one-half cup of butter or margarine, which contains about 800 calories, your savings in calories are clearly tremendous. Even more calories are eliminated when the purée is used to replace oil, which has about 960 calories per half cup. Just as important, you're replacing a high-fat ingredient with one that contains no fat.

While Prune Purée isn't available in stores, you can make it quickly and easily in your own kitchen. (See the inset on page 143.) And when time is a problem, you can try using Wonder-Slim fat substitute, which is interchangeable with Prune Purée.

Prune Butter has a pronounced fruity flavor that blends well with chocolate and spiced baked goods. When using Prune Butter, you'll replace the fat in your recipe with an equal amount of the prune mixture. What does this mean in terms of calorie savings? Prune Butter has 160 calories per one-fourth cup. The same amount of oil has 480 calories, while butter and many margarines have about 400 calories. And because the sweetness of Prune Butter allows you to use less sugar, you'll be saving calories in two ways.

Like Prune Purée, Prune Butter is easily made at home. (See page 143.) When time is short, you can use a prepared butter found in the jam and jelly section of many supermarkets. Keep in mind, though, that most commercial brands of this spread contain added corn syrup (sugar), while your homemade Prune Butter will contain no added sugar.

GETTING THE FAT OUT

Below, you'll find easy-to-follow guidelines that will help you replace the fats in your own recipes. (For more helpful hints on modifying favorite recipes, see the inset on page 22.) In the inset on page 143, you'll find recipes for Prune Purée and Prune Butter—the two fat replacements used throughout this chapter. The remainder of the chapter presents kitchen-tested recipes for a variety of muffins, quick breads, scones, cakes, cookies, pies, and brownies made moist and luscious with prunes.

USING PRUNE PURÉE

CAKE, MUFFIN, AND QUICK BREAD RECIPES

▓ Replace all or part of the butter, margarine, or other solid shortening in cake, muffin, and quick bread recipes with half as much Prune Purée. If the recipe calls for oil, replace all or part of the oil with three-fourths as much Prune Purée.

▓ When eliminating all of the fat from a recipe, reduce the number of eggs by half, or substitute 1 egg white for each whole egg in the recipe. In some recipes—quick bread and chocolate cake recipes, for instance—each whole egg can successfully be replaced with 2 tablespoons of Prune Purée.

▓ To retain moistness, bake fat-free and fat-reduced cakes, muffins, and quick breads at a slightly lower-than-standard temperature. Bake muffins at 350°F. Bake quick breads and cakes at 325°F to 350°F. *Be careful not to overbake.* Bake just until a wooden toothpick inserted in the center comes out clean.

BISCUIT AND SCONE RECIPES

▓ Replace all or part of the butter, margarine, or other solid shortening in biscuit and scone recipes with half as much Prune Purée. If the recipe calls for oil, replace all or part of the oil with three-fourths as much Prune Purée.

▓ When eliminating all of the fat from a biscuit or scone recipe, reduce the number of eggs by half, or substitute 1 egg white for each whole egg.

▓ Bake fat-free biscuits and scones at 375°F.

BROWNIE RECIPES

▓ Replace all or part of the butter, margarine, or other solid shortening in brownie recipes with half as much Prune Purée. If the recipe calls for oil, replace all or part of the oil with three-fourths as much Prune Purée.

▓ When eliminating all of the fat from a brownie recipe, you may replace each whole egg with 3 tablespoons of fat-free egg substitute if desired. However, it is not necessary to reduce the number of eggs.

▓ Bake fat-free brownies at 325°F to 350°F, and check for doneness a few minutes before the end of the usual baking time. Remove the brownies from the oven as soon as the edges are firm and the center is almost set.

COOKIE RECIPES

▓ Replace all or part of the butter, margarine, or other solid shortening in cookie recipes with half as much Prune Purée. If the recipe calls for oil, replace all or part of the oil with three-fourths as much Prune Purée.

- To give your cookies the best texture, replace one-half to three-fourths of the fat with Prune Purée, and replace the remaining fat with a liquid sweetener. (See Chapter 4 for information on using liquid sweeteners.) Substitute 2 tablespoons of Prune Purée for each egg in the recipe.

- Before baking, flatten the cookies slightly with the tip of a spoon to aid spreading. If the cookies still do not spread satisfactorily, you may have to increase the baking soda by 25 percent.

- When baking fat-free and fat-reduced cookies, use the standard oven temperature and baking time.

CRUMB CRUST RECIPES

- Replace all of the butter, margarine, or other solid shortening in sweet crumb crusts—graham cracker and cereal crusts, for instance—with half as much Prune Purée. If the recipe calls for oil, replace all or part of the oil with three-fourths as much Prune Purée. Mix up the crust. The mixture should look like moist, loose crumbs, and should hold together when pinched.

- Form the crust by using the back of a spoon to pat the mixture into a pie pan that has been coated with nonstick cooking spray. Periodically dip the spoon in sugar to prevent sticking.

- Bake fat-free crumb crusts at 350°F just until the edges feel firm and dry. Cool and fill as desired.

CRUMB TOPPING RECIPES

- Replace all of the butter, margarine, or other solid shortening in crumb toppings with half as much Prune Purée.

USING PRUNE BUTTER

CAKE, MUFFIN, AND QUICK BREAD RECIPES

- Replace all or part of the butter, margarine, or other solid shortening in cake, muffin, and quick bread recipes with an equal amount of Prune Butter. To prevent the baked goods from being overly sweet, reduce the amount of sugar in the recipe by one-half to two-thirds the amount of Prune Butter being used.

▓ When eliminating all of the fat from a recipe, reduce the number of eggs by half, or substitute 1 egg white for each whole egg in the recipe. In some recipes, you may be able to eliminate the eggs altogether by replacing each whole egg with 2 tablespoons of water or another liquid.

▓ When baking fat-free and fat-reduced cakes, muffins, and quick breads, use the standard oven temperature and baking time.

Scone Recipes

▓ Replace all or part of the butter, margarine, or other solid shortening in scone recipes with an equal amount of Prune Butter. To prevent the scones from being overly sweet, reduce the amount of sugar in the recipe by one-half to two-thirds the amount of Prune Butter being used.

▓ When eliminating all of the fat from a scone recipe, you may replace each whole egg with 3 tablespoons of fat-free egg substitute if desired. However, it is not necessary to reduce the number of eggs.

▓ Bake fat-free scones at 375°F.

Brownie Recipes

▓ Replace all or part of the butter, margarine, or other solid shortening in brownie recipes with an equal amount of Prune Butter. To prevent the brownies from being overly sweet, reduce the amount of sugar in the recipe by one-half to two-thirds the amount of Prune Butter being used.

▓ When eliminating all of the fat from a brownie recipe, you may replace each whole egg with 3 tablespoons of fat-free egg substitute. However, it is not necessary to reduce the number of eggs.

▓ Bake fat-free brownies at 325°F to 350°F, and check for doneness a few minutes before the end of the usual baking time. Remove the brownies from the oven as soon as the edges are firm and the center is almost set.

COOKIE RECIPES

▓ Replace all or part of the butter, margarine, or other solid shortening in cookie recipes with an equal amount of Prune Butter. To prevent the baked goods from being overly sweet, reduce the amount of sugar in the recipe by one-half to two-thirds the amount of Prune Butter being used.

▓ When eliminating all of the fat from a cookie recipe, you may replace each whole egg with 3 tablespoons of fat-free egg substitute if desired. However, it is not necessary to reduce the number of eggs.

▓ When baking fat-free and fat-reduced cookies, use the standard oven temperature and baking time.

CRUMB CRUST RECIPES

▓ Replace all of the butter, margarine, or other solid shortening in sweet crumb crusts—graham cracker and cereal crusts, for instance—with an equal amount of Prune Butter. To prevent the crust from being overly sweet, reduce the sugar by one-half to two-thirds the amount of Prune Butter being used. Mix up the crust. The mixture should look like moist, loose crumbs, and should hold together when pinched.

▓ Form the crust by using the back of a spoon to pat the mixture into a pie pan that has been coated with nonstick cooking spray. Periodically dip the spoon in sugar to prevent sticking.

▓ Bake fat-free crumb crusts at 350°F just until the edges feel firm and dry. Cool and fill as desired.

CRUMB TOPPING RECIPES

▓ Replace all of the butter, margarine, or other solid shortening in crumb toppings with an equal amount of Prune Butter. Reduce the sugar in the recipe by one-half to two-thirds the amount of Prune Butter being used.

MAKING PRUNE PURÉE AND PRUNE BUTTER

Prune Purée and Prune Butter allow you to make moist and flavorful baked goods with little or no fat. These wonderful fat substitutes also add fiber and nutrients to cakes, muffins, cookies, and other sweet treats. Simply follow the recipes provided below, and keep Prune Purée and Prune Butter on hand to reduce the fat and boost the nutrition of all your baked goods.

RUNE PURÉE

Yield: 1-1/2 cups   3 ounces pitted prunes (about 1/2 cup)
1 cup water or fruit juice
2 teaspoons lecithin granules*

1 Place all ingredients in a blender or food processor, and process at high speed until the mixture is smooth.

2 Use immediately, or place in an airtight container and store for up to 3 weeks in the refrigerator.

* For information on lecithin, see the inset on page 83.

RUNE BUTTER

Yield: 1 cup   8 ounces pitted prunes (about 1-1/3 cups)
6 tablespoons water or fruit juice

1 Place all ingredients in a food processor, and process at high speed until the mixture is a smooth paste. (Note that this mixture is too thick to be made in a blender.)

2 Use immediately, or place in an airtight container and store for up to 3 weeks in the refrigerator.

STRAWBERRY OATMEAL MUFFINS

Yield: 12 muffins

NUTRITIONAL FACTS
(PER MUFFIN)
CALORIES: 120
FAT: 0.9 G
PROTEIN: 4.6 G
CHOLESTEROL: 0 MG
SODIUM: 136 MG
FIBER: 2.9 G
CALCIUM: 55 MG
POTASSIUM: 154 MG
IRON: 0.9 MG

1-1/4 cups quick-cooking oats

1-1/4 cups nonfat buttermilk

1-1/4 cups whole wheat flour

1/3 cup sugar

1 tablespoon baking powder

1/4 teaspoon baking soda

2 tablespoons plus 1-1/2 teaspoons
 Prune Purée (page 143)

2 egg whites

1 teaspoon vanilla extract

1 cup chopped fresh or frozen strawberries

Topping:

1 tablespoon sugar

1 Combine the oats and buttermilk, stir to mix well, and set aside for at least 5 minutes.

2 Combine the flour, sugar, baking powder, and baking soda, and stir to mix well. Add the oat-buttermilk mixture, Prune Purée, egg whites, and vanilla extract, and stir just until the dry ingredients are moistened. Fold in the strawberries.

3 Coat muffin cups with nonstick cooking spray, and fill 3/4 full with the batter. Sprinkle 1/4 teaspoon of sugar over the top of each muffin. Bake at 350°F for 15 to 17 minutes, or just until a wooden toothpick inserted in the center of a muffin comes out clean.

4 Remove the muffin tin from the oven, and allow it to sit for 5 minutes before removing the muffins. Serve warm or at room temperature.

FANTASTIC FRUIT MUFFINS

Yield: 12 muffins

3/4 cup quick-cooking oats

3/4 cup skim milk

1-1/2 cups whole wheat flour

1/4 cup plus 2 tablespoons brown sugar

1 tablespoon baking powder

1/4 teaspoon baking soda

2 tablespoons plus 1-1/2 teaspoons
Prune Purée (page 143)

2 egg whites

1 teaspoon vanilla extract

1 cup finely chopped fresh pears
(about 1-1/2 medium)

1/3 cup coarsely chopped fresh or frozen
cranberries

1/3 cup golden raisins

1 Combine the oats and skim milk, stir to mix well, and set aside for at least 5 minutes.

2 Combine the flour, brown sugar, baking powder, and baking soda, and stir to mix well. Add the oat-milk mixture and the Prune Purée, egg whites, vanilla extract, and pears, and stir just until the dry ingredients are moistened. Fold in the cranberries and raisins.

3 Coat muffin cups with nonstick cooking spray, and fill 3/4 full with the batter. Bake at 350°F for 15 to 17 minutes, or just until a wooden toothpick inserted in the center of a muffin comes out clean.

4 Remove the muffin tin from the oven, and allow it to sit for 5 minutes before removing the muffins. Serve warm or at room temperature.

PEACH PERFECTION MUFFINS

Yield: 12 muffins

NUTRITIONAL FACTS (PER MUFFIN)
CALORIES: 115
FAT: 0.8 G
PROTEIN: 4 G
CHOLESTEROL: 0 MG
SODIUM: 98 MG
FIBER: 3.3 G
CALCIUM: 40 MG
POTASSIUM: 184 MG
IRON: 1 MG

1 cup whole wheat flour

1 cup oat bran

1 tablespoon baking powder

1/4 cup plus 2 tablespoons honey

1/4 cup plus 2 tablespoons plain nonfat yogurt

3 tablespoons Prune Purée (page 143)

2 egg whites

1 teaspoon vanilla extract

1 cup chopped fresh peaches (about 2 medium)

1/3 cup chopped dried dates or raisins

1 Combine the flour, oat bran, and baking powder, and stir to mix well. Add the honey, yogurt, Prune Purée, egg whites, and vanilla extract, and stir just until the dry ingredients are moistened. Fold in the peaches and the dates or raisins.

2 Coat muffin cups with nonstick cooking spray, and fill 3/4 full with the batter. Bake at 350°F for 15 to 17 minutes, or just until a wooden toothpick inserted in the center of a muffin comes out clean.

3 Remove the muffin tin from the oven, and allow it to sit for 5 minutes before removing the muffins. Serve warm or at room temperature.

CARROT PINEAPPLE MUFFINS

Yield: 12 muffins

NUTRITIONAL FACTS (PER MUFFIN)
CALORIES: 133
FAT: 0.4 G
PROTEIN: 3.6 G
CHOLESTEROL: 0 MG
SODIUM: 81 MG
FIBER: 3.2 G
CALCIUM: 14 MG
POTASSIUM: 170 MG
IRON: 1 MG

2 cups whole wheat flour

1/2 cup sugar

1 teaspoon baking soda

1/2 teaspoon ground cinnamon

1 can (8 ounces) crushed pineapple packed in juice, undrained

1/4 cup Prune Purée (page 143)

2 egg whites

1 teaspoon vanilla extract

1/2 cup (packed) grated carrots (about 1 medium)

1/3 cup raisins or chopped pecans

1. Combine the flour, sugar, baking soda, and cinnamon, and stir to mix well. Add the pineapple, including the juice, and the Prune Purée, egg whites, and vanilla extract, and stir just until the dry ingredients are moistened. Fold in the carrots and the raisins or pecans.

2. Coat muffin cups with nonstick cooking spray, and fill 3/4 full with the batter. Bake at 350°F for 15 to 17 minutes, or just until a wooden toothpick inserted in the center of a muffin comes out clean.

3. Remove the muffin tin from the oven, and allow it to sit for 5 minutes before removing the muffins. Serve warm or at room temperature.

WHOLE WHEAT BANANA BREAD

Yield: 16 slices

NUTRITIONAL FACTS
(PER SLICE)

CALORIES: 92

FAT: 0.3 G

PROTEIN: 2.2 G

CHOLESTEROL: 0 MG

SODIUM: 74 MG

FIBER: 2.3 G

CALCIUM: 15 MG

POTASSIUM: 169 MG

IRON: 0.9 MG

2 cups whole wheat flour

1 teaspoon baking soda

1 teaspoon baking powder

1/4 cup plus 2 tablespoons sugar

1-1/2 cups mashed very ripe banana
   (about 3 large)

1/4 cup Prune Purée (page 143)

1 teaspoon vanilla extract

1/3 cup chopped walnuts (optional)

1 Combine the flour, baking soda, baking powder, and sugar, and stir to mix well. Add the banana, Prune Purée, and vanilla extract, and stir just until the dry ingredients are moistened. Fold in the walnuts if desired.

2 Coat an 8-x-4-inch loaf pan with nonstick cooking spray. Spread the mixture evenly in the pan, and bake at 350°F for about 50 minutes, or just until a wooden toothpick inserted in the center of the loaf comes out clean.

3 Remove the bread from the oven, and let sit for 10 minutes. Invert the loaf onto a wire rack, turn right side up, and cool before slicing and serving.

CINNAMON RAISIN BREAD

Yield: 16 slices

NUTRITIONAL FACTS
(PER SLICE)

CALORIES: 93	
FAT: 0.5 G	
PROTEIN: 2.8 G	
CHOLESTEROL: 0 MG	
SODIUM: 90 MG	
FIBER: 2.3 G	
CALCIUM: 36 MG	
POTASSIUM: 146 MG	
IRON: 1 MG	

2 cups whole wheat flour

1/3 cup brown sugar

1 teaspoon baking soda

1 teaspoon baking powder

2 teaspoons ground cinnamon

1 cup nonfat buttermilk

1/4 cup Prune Purée (page 143)

1 teaspoon vanilla extract

1/2 cup dark raisins

1 Combine the flour, brown sugar, baking soda, baking powder, and cinnamon, and stir to mix well. Add the buttermilk, Prune Purée, and vanilla extract, and stir just until the dry ingredients are moistened. Fold in the raisins.

2 Coat an 8-x-4-inch loaf pan with nonstick cooking spray. Spread the mixture evenly in the pan, and bake at 350°F for about 45 minutes, or just until a wooden toothpick inserted in the center of the loaf comes out clean.

3 Remove the bread from the oven, and let sit for 10 minutes. Invert the loaf onto a wire rack, turn right side up, and cool before slicing and serving.

PRUNE AND ORANGE BREAD

Yield: 16 slices

NUTRITIONAL FACTS
(PER SLICE)

CALORIES: 82	
FAT: 0.3 G	
PROTEIN: 2.4 G	
CHOLESTEROL: 0 MG	
SODIUM: 73 MG	
FIBER: 3 G	
CALCIUM: 15 MG	
POTASSIUM: 162 MG	
IRON: 0.9 MG	

2 cups whole wheat flour

1 teaspoon baking soda

1 teaspoon baking powder

1 teaspoon dried grated orange rind, or
    1 tablespoon fresh

3/4 cup Prune Butter (page 143)

3/4 cup orange juice

1/3 cup chopped pecans (optional)

1 Combine the flour, baking soda, baking powder, and orange peel, and stir to mix well. Add the Prune Butter and orange juice, and stir just until the dry ingredients are moistened. Fold in the pecans if desired.

2 Coat an 8-x-4-inch loaf pan with non-stick cooking spray. Spread the mixture evenly in the pan, and bake at 350°F for about 40 minutes, or just until a wooden toothpick inserted in the center of the loaf comes out clean.

3 Remove the bread from the oven, and let sit for 10 minutes. Invert the loaf onto a wire rack, turn right side up, and cool before slicing and serving.

RUITFUL SCONES

Yield: 12 scones

NUTRITIONAL FACTS
(PER SCONE)

CALORIES: 103	
FAT: 0.3 G	
PROTEIN: 3.9 G	
CHOLESTEROL: 0 MG	
SODIUM: 81 MG	
FIBER: 1.6 G	
CALCIUM: 38 MG	
POTASSIUM: 114 MG	
IRON: 1.1 MG	

1-1/2 cups unbleached flour
3/4 cup whole wheat flour
3/4 teaspoon baking soda
1/2 teaspoon baking powder
1/4 cup plus 2 tablespoons Prune Butter (page 143)
1 egg white
3/4 cup plain nonfat yogurt
1/4 cup dark raisins or dried cranberries
1/4 cup chopped walnuts or pecans (optional)
Skim milk
Cinnamon sugar (optional)

1. Combine the flours, baking soda, and baking powder, and stir to mix well. In a separate bowl, combine the Prune Butter, egg white, and yogurt, and stir to mix well. Add just enough of the prune mixture to the flour mixture to form a stiff dough. Stir in the raisins or cranberries and the nuts if desired.

2. Form the dough into a ball, and turn onto a lightly floured surface. With floured hands, pat the dough into a 7-inch circle.

3. Coat a baking sheet with nonstick cooking spray. Place the dough on the sheet, and use a sharp floured knife to cut it into 12 wedges. Pull the wedges out slightly to leave a 1/2-inch space between them. Brush the tops lightly with skim milk, and sprinkle with cinnamon sugar if desired.

4. Bake at 375°F for 18 to 20 minutes, or until golden brown. Transfer to a serving plate, and serve hot.

MOCHA FUDGE CAKE

Yield: 16 servings

2 cups unbleached flour

1-1/4 cups sugar

1/2 cup cocoa powder

1 teaspoon baking powder

1/2 teaspoon baking soda

1/4 teaspoon salt (optional)

3/4 cup Prune Butter (page 143)

1-1/2 cups plus 2 tablespoons coffee, at room temperature

2 teaspoons vanilla extract

1/2 cup chopped walnuts (optional)

3–4 tablespoons confectioners' sugar (optional)

1 Combine the flour, sugar, cocoa, baking powder, baking soda, and salt, if desired, and stir to mix well. In a separate bowl, combine the Prune Butter, coffee, and vanilla extract, and stir to mix well. Add the prune mixture to the flour mixture, and stir to mix well. Fold in the walnuts if desired.

2 Coat a 9-x-13-inch pan with nonstick cooking spray. Spread the batter evenly in the pan, and bake at 350°F for 30 to 35 minutes, or until the top springs back when lightly touched and a wooden toothpick inserted in the center of the cake comes out clean. Be careful not to overbake.

3 Cool the cake to room temperature. Sift the confectioners' sugar over the cake if desired, cut into squares, and serve.

EAR CRUMBLE CAKE

Yield: 8 servings

2/3 cup unbleached flour

2/3 cup whole wheat flour

1/2 cup sugar

1-1/2 teaspoons baking powder

1/8 teaspoon ground nutmeg

2/3 cup skim milk

1/4 cup Prune Purée (page 143)

1 egg white

1-1/2 cups sliced peeled fresh pears (about 1-1/2 medium)

Topping:

1/4 cup quick-cooking oats

2 tablespoons toasted wheat germ

2 tablespoons brown sugar

1 tablespoon maple syrup

1 To make the topping, stir the topping ingredients together until moist and crumbly. Set aside.

2 Combine the flours, sugar, baking powder, and nutmeg, and stir to mix well. Stir in the milk, Prune Purée, and egg white.

3 Coat a 9-inch round pan with nonstick cooking spray. Spread the batter evenly in the pan, and arrange the pear slices in a circular pattern over the batter. Sprinkle the topping over the pear slices.

4 Bake at 350°F for 30 to 35 minutes, or until a wooden toothpick inserted in the center of the cake comes out clean.

5 Cool the cake for at least 20 minutes. Cut into wedges and serve warm or at room temperature.

PRUNE AND APPLE COFFEE CAKE

Yield: 8 servings

NUTRITIONAL FACTS
(PER SERVING)

CALORIES: 170

FAT: 0.9 G

PROTEIN: 5 G

CHOLESTEROL: 0 MG

SODIUM: 99 MG

FIBER: 3 G

CALCIUM: 51 MG

POTASSIUM: 237 MG

IRON: 1.6 MG

1 cup unbleached flour

1/2 cup oat bran

1/4 cup sugar

1/2 teaspoon baking powder

1/2 teaspoon baking soda

1/2 cup Prune Butter (page 143)

2 egg whites

1/2 cup plain nonfat yogurt

1 teaspoon vanilla extract

Filling:

3/4 cup finely chopped fresh apples
(about 1 medium)

2 tablespoons brown sugar

1/4 teaspoon ground cinnamon

Topping:

1 tablespoon brown sugar

2 teaspoons finely ground walnuts

1 To make the filling, combine the apple, brown sugar, and cinnamon, and stir to mix well. Set aside.

2 To make the topping, combine the brown sugar and walnuts until crumbly. Set aside.

3 Combine the flour, oat bran, sugar, baking powder, and baking soda, and stir to mix well. Add the remaining ingredients, and stir to mix well.

4 Coat an 8-inch round pan with nonstick cooking spray. Spread half of the batter evenly in the pan. Arrange the filling over the batter, and spread the remaining batter over the filling. Sprinkle the topping over the batter.

5 Bake at 350°F for 30 to 35 minutes, or until the top springs back when lightly touched and a wooden toothpick inserted in the center of the cake comes out clean.

6 Cool the cake for at least 20 minutes. Cut into wedges and serve warm or at room temperature.

𝒫RUNE-THE-FAT PIE CRUST

Yield: One 9-inch pie crust for 8 servings

NUTRITIONAL FACTS (PER SERVING)
CALORIES: 86
FAT: 0.2 G
PROTEIN: 1.5 G
CHOLESTEROL: 0 MG
SODIUM: 126 MG
FIBER: 1.8 G
CALCIUM: 8 MG
POTASSIUM: 79 MG
IRON: 0.7 MG

8 large (2-1/2-x-5-inch) fat-free graham crackers

2 tablespoons sugar

2 tablespoons Prune Purée (page 143)

1 Break the crackers in pieces, and place in the bowl of a food processor or in a blender. Process into fine crumbs. Measure the crumbs.

2 Return the crumbs—approximately 1-1/4 cups—to the food processor, and add sugar and Prune Purée. Process until moist and crumbly.

3 Coat a 9-inch pie pan with nonstick cooking spray. Use back of spoon to press the crumbs against the sides and bottom of the pan, forming an even crust. Periodically dip the spoon in sugar to prevent sticking.

4 Bake the pie shell at 350°F for 10 minutes, or until the edges feel firm and dry. Cool the crust to room temperature, and fill as desired.

PLUM DELICIOUS PIE CRUST

Yield: One 9-inch pie crust for 8 servings

NUTRITIONAL FACTS (PER SERVING)
CALORIES: 89
FAT: 0.2 G
PROTEIN: 1.7 G
CHOLESTEROL: 0 MG
SODIUM: 126 MG
FIBER: 1.1 G
CALCIUM: 11 MG
POTASSIUM: 125 MG
IRON: 0.8 MG

If you can't find a fat-free brand of graham crackers, just use regular graham crackers. All graham crackers are quite low in fat.

8 large (2-1/2-x-5-inch) fat-free graham crackers

1/4 cup Prune Butter (page 143)

1 Break the crackers in pieces, and place in the bowl of a food processor or in a blender. Process into fine crumbs. Measure the crumbs. There should be 1-1/4 cups.

2 Return the crumbs to the food processor, and add the Prune Butter. Process until moist and crumbly.

3 Coat a 9-inch pie pan with nonstick cooking spray. Use the back of a spoon to press the crumbs against the sides and bottom of the pan, forming an even crust. Periodically dip the spoon in sugar to prevent sticking.

4 Bake the pie shell at 350°F for 10 minutes, or until the edges feel firm and dry. Cool the crust to room temperature, and fill as desired.

FRESH NECTARINE PIE

Yield: 8 servings

NUTRITIONAL FACTS
(PER SERVING)

CALORIES: 199

FAT: 0.3 G

PROTEIN: 2.7 G

CHOLESTEROL: 0 MG

SODIUM: 127 MG

FIBER: 2.4 G

CALCIUM: 21 MG

POTASSIUM: 360 MG

IRON: 1 MG

This pie is equally good when made with strawberries, peaches, or other fruits.

1 prepared Plum Delicious Pie Crust
   (page 156)

Glaze:

1/3 cup sugar

3 tablespoons cornstarch

1-1/2 cups orange juice

Filling:

4 cups sliced peeled fresh nectarines
   (about 4 medium)

1 To make the glaze, combine the sugar and cornstarch in a medium-sized saucepan. Slowly stir in the orange juice. Place over medium heat and cook, stirring constantly, until the glaze mixture is thickened and bubbly. Remove the saucepan from the heat, and set aside for 20 minutes.

2 Spoon a thin layer of the glaze over the bottom of the pie crust. Arrange half of the nectarine slices over the bottom of the crust. Spoon half of the remaining glaze over the nectarine slices. Arrange the rest of the nectarine slices over the glaze, and top with the remaining glaze.

3 Chill for several hours, or until the glaze is set. Cut into wedges and serve cold or at room temperature.

LEMON CHEESE PIE

Yield: 8 servings

NUTRITIONAL FACTS
(PER SERVING)

CALORIES: 220

FAT: 0.2 G

PROTEIN: 4.6 G

CHOLESTEROL: 0 MG

SODIUM: 203 MG

FIBER: 1.8 G

CALCIUM: 76 MG

POTASSIUM: 184 MG

IRON: 1 MG

3/4 cup sugar

1/2 cup cornstarch

1-3/4 cups nonfat buttermilk

1 tablespoon freshly grated lemon rind

1/2 cup fat-free egg substitute

1/3 cup fresh lemon juice

1 prepared Prune-the-Fat Pie Crust
   (page 155)

1 Combine the sugar and cornstarch in a medium-sized nonstick saucepan. Slowly stir in the buttermilk. Place over medium heat and cook, constantly stirring with a wire whisk, until the mixture is thickened and bubbly. Add the lemon rind to the buttermilk mixture, and continue to cook and stir for another minute or 2.

2 Reduce the heat to low, and blend about 1/2 cup of the hot mixture into the egg substitute. Then return the egg mixture to the pan. Cook and stir over low heat for 2 to 3 additional minutes. Do not allow the mixture to come to a boil.

3 Remove the mixture from the heat, and stir in the lemon juice. Pour the filling into the pie crust.

4 Chill for several hours, or until the filling is set. Cut into wedges and serve cold.

BANANA CREAM PIE

Yield: 8 servings

NUTRITIONAL FACTS
(PER SERVING)
CALORIES: 211
FAT: 0.3 G
PROTEIN: 5 G
CHOLESTEROL: 0 MG
SODIUM: 173 MG
FIBER: 1.3 G
CALCIUM: 90 MG
POTASSIUM: 358 MG
IRON: 1.1 MG

1/2 cup sugar

3 tablespoons cornstarch

1 pinch ground nutmeg

2 cups skim milk

1/4 cup plus 2 tablespoons fat-free egg substitute

1 teaspoon vanilla extract

1 prepared Prune-the-Fat Pie Crust (page 155)

3 large bananas, sliced 1/4 inch thick

Ground nutmeg (optional)

1 Combine the sugar, cornstarch, and nutmeg in a medium-sized saucepan. Slowly stir in the milk. Place over medium heat and cook, stirring constantly with a wire whisk, until the mixture comes to a boil. Reduce the heat to low, and cook and stir for another minute or 2.

2 Blend about 1/2 cup of the hot mixture into the egg substitute. Then return the egg mixture to the pan. Cook and stir over low heat for 2 to 3 minutes. Do not allow the mixture to come to a boil.

3 Remove the mixture from the heat, and stir in the vanilla extract. Let the mixture cool for 15 minutes, stirring every 5 minutes.

4 Spread a thin layer of the filling over the bottom of the pie crust. Top with half of the bananas and half of the remaining filling. Repeat the layers, ending with the filling. Sprinkle the top lightly with ground nutmeg if desired.

5 Chill for several hours, or until the filling is set. Cut into wedges and serve cold.

RAZZLEBERRY PIE

Yield: 8 servings

NUTRITIONAL FACTS
(PER SERVING)

CALORIES: 195

FAT: 0.4 G

PROTEIN: 3.3 G

CHOLESTEROL: 0 MG

SODIUM: 144 MG

FIBER: 3.2 G

CALCIUM: 62 MG

POTASSIUM: 256 MG

IRON: 1.1 MG

This pie is equally delicious when made with the Prune-the-Fat Pie Crust.

1/4 cup sugar

1/4 cup cornstarch

1 cup cran-raspberry juice or other raspberry juice blend

1 cup nonfat raspberry yogurt

1 cup sliced fresh strawberries

1 cup fresh blueberries

1 cup fresh raspberries

1 prepared Plum Delicious Pie Crust (page 156)

1 Combine the sugar and cornstarch in a medium-sized saucepan. Slowly stir in the juice. Then stir in the yogurt. Place over medium heat and cook, stirring constantly with a wire whisk, until the mixture comes to a boil. Reduce the heat to low, and cook and stir for another minute or 2. Remove the mixture from the heat, and set aside for 15 minutes.

2 Combine the fruits. Spread a thin layer of the filling over the bottom of the pie crust. Top with half of the fruit and half of the remaining filling. Repeat the layers, ending with the filling.

3 Chill for several hours, or until the filling is set. Cut into wedges and serve cold.

BLUEBERRY CHEESECAKE

Yield: 10 servings

NUTRITIONAL FACTS
(PER SERVING)

CALORIES: 215

FAT: 0.1 G

PROTEIN: 13.5 G

CHOLESTEROL: 4 MG

SODIUM: 290 MG

FIBER: 0.9 G

CALCIUM: 396 MG

POTASSIUM: 112 MG

IRON: 1 MG

1 recipe Prune-the-Fat Pie Crust (page 155)
8 ounces nonfat cream cheese
15 ounces nonfat ricotta cheese
1/2 cup fat-free egg substitute
2 teaspoons vanilla extract
1 tablespoon fresh lemon juice
1/3 cup unbleached flour
3/4 cup sugar
3/4 cup fresh or frozen blueberries

1. Coat a 9-inch springform pan with nonstick cooking spray. Prepare the graham cracker crust as directed, but pat it over the bottom of the pan and 3/4-inch up the side. Bake at 350°F for 8 to 9 minutes, or until the edges feel firm and dry. Set aside to cool.

2. Place the remaining ingredients, except for the blueberries, in a food processor or blender, and process until smooth. Fold in the blueberries.

3. Pour the filling into the crust. Bake at 350°F for about 50 minutes, or until the crust is lightly browned around the edges and the filling is set.

4. Turn the oven off, and let the cake cool in the oven with the door ajar for 1 hour. Refrigerate for at least 8 hours, cut into wedges, and serve.

FRUITFUL BREAKFAST BARS

Yield: 10 servings

NUTRITIONAL FACTS (PER SERVING)
CALORIES: 128
FAT: 0.9 G
PROTEIN: 4.1 G
CHOLESTEROL: 0 MG
SODIUM: 25 MG
FIBER: 3.1 G
CALCIUM: 19 MG
POTASSIUM: 256 MG
IRON: 1.6 MG

Two of these bars plus a glass of milk make a quick and nutritious breakfast.

3/4 cup whole wheat flour

1/2 cup toasted wheat germ

1/4 cup quick-cooking oats

1/2 teaspoon baking powder

1/2 teaspoon ground cinnamon

1/4 cup Prune Butter (page 143)

1/4 cup honey or molasses

3 tablespoons fat-free egg substitute

1/2 cup dark raisins

1/2 cup chopped dried apricots

1 Combine the flour, wheat germ, oats, baking powder, and cinnamon, and stir to mix well. Add the Prune Butter, honey or molasses, and egg substitute, and stir to mix well. Fold in the raisins and apricots.

2 Coat an 8-inch square pan with nonstick cooking spray. Spread the mixture evenly in the pan, and bake at 350°F for about 25 minutes, or until lightly browned.

3 Cool to room temperature, cut into bars, and serve.

VERY BEST FUDGE BROWNIES

Yield: 36 servings

4 squares (1 ounce each) unsweetened baking chocolate

1-1/2 cups sugar

1/2 cup plus 1 tablespoon fat-free egg substitute

3/4 cup Prune Butter (page 143)

2 teaspoons vanilla extract

1 cup unbleached flour

1/4 teaspoon salt (optional)

3/4 cup chopped walnuts (optional)

1 If using a microwave oven to melt the chocolate, place the chocolate in a mixing bowl and microwave uncovered at high power for 3 to 4 minutes, or until almost melted. Remove the bowl from the oven and stir the chocolate until completely melted. If melting the chocolate on the stove top, place the chocolate in a small saucepan and cook over low heat, stirring constantly, until melted.

2 Add the sugar, egg substitute, Prune Butter, and vanilla extract to the chocolate, and stir to mix well. Stir in the flour and, if desired, the salt and nuts.

3 Coat a 9-x-13-inch pan with nonstick cooking spray. Spread the batter evenly in the pan, and bake at 325°F for 35 to 40 minutes, or until the edges are firm and the center is almost set.

4 Cool to room temperature, cut into squares, and serve.

VERY BEST CAKE BROWNIES

Yield: 36 servings

NUTRITIONAL FACTS (PER SERVING)
CALORIES: 90
FAT: 1.7 G
PROTEIN: 1.7 G
CHOLESTEROL: 0 MG
SODIUM: 32 MG
FIBER: 1.3 G
CALCIUM: 6 MG
POTASSIUM: 87 MG
IRON: 0.8 MG

4 squares (1 ounce each) unsweetened baking chocolate

1-1/2 cups sugar

1/2 cup plus 1 tablespoon fat-free egg substitute

1/2 cup skim milk

3/4 cup Prune Butter (page 143)

2 teaspoons vanilla extract

1-1/2 cups unbleached flour

1/4 teaspoon salt (optional)

3/4 cup chopped walnuts (optional)

1 If using a microwave oven to melt the chocolate, place the chocolate in a mixing bowl and microwave uncovered at high power for 3 to 4 minutes, or until almost melted. Remove the bowl from the oven and stir the chocolate until completely melted. If melting the chocolate on the stove top, place the chocolate in a small saucepan and cook over low heat, stirring constantly, until melted.

2 Add the sugar, egg substitute, milk, Prune Butter, and vanilla extract to the chocolate, and stir to mix well. Stir in the flour and, if desired, the salt and nuts.

3 Coat a 9-x-13-inch pan with nonstick cooking spray. Spread the batter evenly in the pan, and bake at 325°F for 35 to 40 minutes, or until the center springs back when lightly touched.

4 Cool to room temperature, cut into squares, and serve.

FUDGY COCOA BROWNIES

Yield: 16 servings

NUTRITIONAL FACTS
(PER SERVING)

CALORIES: 76	
FAT: 0.5 G	
PROTEIN: 1.5 G	
CHOLESTEROL: 0 MG	
SODIUM: 23 MG	
FIBER: 1.6 G	
CALCIUM: 10 MG	
POTASSIUM: 82 MG	
IRON: 0.8 MG	

1/2 cup Prune Butter (page 143)

3/4 cup sugar

3 egg whites

1/4 cup plus 2 tablespoons cocoa powder

1/4 cup plus 2 tablespoons unbleached
flour

1/4 cup oat bran

1/8 teaspoon salt (optional)

1 teaspoon vanilla extract

1/3 cup chopped nuts (optional)

1 Combine the Prune Butter, sugar, and egg whites, and stir to mix well. Add the remaining ingredients and stir well.

2 Coat an 8-inch square pan with nonstick cooking spray. Spread the batter evenly in the pan, and bake at 325°F for 23 to 25 minutes, or until the edges are firm and the center is almost set.

3 Cool to room temperature, cut into squares, and serve.

MILK CHOCOLATE BROWNIES

Yield: 16 servings

NUTRITIONAL FACTS
(PER SERVING)

CALORIES: 78	
FAT: 0.5 G	
PROTEIN: 1.9 G	
CHOLESTEROL: 0 MG	
SODIUM: 29 MG	
FIBER: 1.4 G	
CALCIUM: 17 MG	
POTASSIUM: 85 MG	
IRON: 0.6 MG	

1/2 cup Prune Butter (page 143)
3/4 cup sugar
3 egg whites
2 teaspoons vanilla extract
1/2 cup unbleached flour
1/4 cup plus 2 tablespoons cocoa powder
3 tablespoons nonfat dry milk
1/8 teaspoon salt (optional)
1/3 cup chopped nuts (optional)

1. Combine the Prune Butter, sugar, egg whites, and vanilla extract, and stir to mix well. Stir in the remaining ingredients.

2. Coat an 8-inch square pan with nonstick cooking spray. Spread the batter evenly in the pan, and bake at 325°F for 25 to 30 minutes, or just until the edges are firm and the center is almost set.

3. Cool to room temperature, cut into squares, and serve.

CHEWY COCONUT BROWNIES

Yield: 16 servings

NUTRITIONAL FACTS (PER SERVING)
CALORIES: 79
FAT: 0.8 G
PROTEIN: 1.5 G
CHOLESTEROL: 0 MG
SODIUM: 24 MG
FIBER: 1 G
CALCIUM: 5 MG
POTASSIUM: 45 MG
IRON: 0.5 MG

1/4 cup plus 2 tablespoons quick-cooking oats

1/4 cup plus 2 tablespoons unbleached flour

1/4 cup plus 2 tablespoons cocoa powder

1 cup sugar

1/8 teaspoon salt (optional)

1/4 cup Prune Purée (page 143)

2 egg whites

1 teaspoon vanilla extract

1 teaspoon coconut-flavored extract

2 tablespoons shredded coconut

1 Combine the oats, flour, cocoa, sugar, and salt, if desired, and stir to mix well. Stir in the Prune Purée, egg whites, and extracts. Fold in the coconut.

2 Coat an 8-inch square pan with nonstick cooking spray. Spread the batter evenly in the pan, and bake at 325°F for about 22 minutes, or until the edges are firm and the center is almost set.

3 Cool to room temperature, cut into squares, and serve.

OATMEAL RAISIN COOKIES

Yield: 40 cookies

NUTRITIONAL FACTS
(PER COOKIE)

CALORIES: 48

FAT: 0.3 G

PROTEIN: 0.7 G

CHOLESTEROL: 0 MG

SODIUM: 21 MG

FIBER: 0.8 G

CALCIUM: 5 MG

POTASSIUM: 43 MG

IRON: 0.3 MG

1 cup whole wheat flour

1-1/2 cups quick-cooking oats

1/2 cup sugar

1 teaspoon baking soda

1/4 cup Prune Purée (page 143)

1/4 cup plus 2 tablespoons honey or molasses

1 teaspoon vanilla extract

1/2 cup dark raisins

1/2 cup chopped walnuts (optional)

1 Combine the flour, oats, sugar, and baking soda, and stir to mix well. Add the Prune Purée, honey or molasses, and vanilla extract, and stir to mix well. (If the dough seems crumbly, keep stirring until it holds together.) Stir in the raisins and nuts if desired.

2 Coat a baking sheet with nonstick cooking spray. Drop rounded teaspoonfuls of dough onto the sheet, placing them 1-1/2 inches apart. Slightly flatten each cookie with the bottom of a glass dipped in sugar.

3 Bake at 350°F for about 9 minutes, or until golden brown. Cool the cookies on the pan for 1 minute. Then transfer the cookies to wire racks, and cool completely. Serve immediately, or transfer to an airtight container and arrange in single layers separated by sheets of waxed paper.

RAISIN AND BRAN JUMBLES

Yield: 42 cookies

NUTRITIONAL FACTS
(PER COOKIE)

CALORIES: 42

FAT: 0.1 G

PROTEIN: 0.8 G

CHOLESTEROL: 0 MG

SODIUM: 36 MG

FIBER: 0.9 G

CALCIUM: 5 MG

POTASSIUM: 58 MG

IRON: 0.6 MG

1 cup plus 2 tablespoons whole wheat flour

3/4 cup sugar

1 teaspoon baking soda

1/4 cup Prune Purée (page 143)

3 tablespoons maple syrup

1 teaspoon vanilla extract

2 cups bran flake-and-raisin cereal

1/3 cup chopped dried apricots

1/3 cup chopped prunes

1 Combine the flour, sugar, and baking soda, and stir to mix well. Add the Prune Purée, maple syrup, and vanilla extract, and stir to mix well. Stir in the cereal, apricots, and prunes.

2 Coat a baking sheet with nonstick cooking spray. Drop rounded teaspoonfuls of dough onto the sheet, placing them 1-1/2 inches apart. Slightly flatten each cookie with the tip of a spoon.

3 Bake at 350°F for about 9 minutes, or until golden brown. Cool the cookies on the pan for 1 minute. Then transfer the cookies to wire racks, and cool completely. Serve immediately, or transfer to an airtight container and arrange in single layers separated by sheets of waxed paper.

CRANBERRY SPICE COOKIES

Yield: 42 cookies

NUTRITIONAL FACTS
(PER COOKIE)

CALORIES: 47

FAT: 0.1 G

PROTEIN: 0.8 G

CHOLESTEROL: 0 MG

SODIUM: 25 MG

FIBER: 0.6 G

CALCIUM: 3 MG

POTASSIUM: 37 MG

IRON: 0.5 MG

1 cup whole wheat flour

3/4 cup plus 2 tablespoons unbleached flour

2/3 cup sugar

1 teaspoon baking soda

1/2 teaspoon ground cinnamon

1/8 teaspoon ground nutmeg

1/4 cup plus 2 tablespoons Prune Purée (page 143)

1/4 cup honey

1 teaspoon vanilla extract

1/2 cup dried cranberries or golden raisins

1 cup oat flakes or other ready-to-eat cereal flakes

1. Combine the flours, sugar, baking soda, and spices, and stir to mix well. Add the Prune Purée, honey, and vanilla extract, and stir to mix well. Stir in the cranberries or raisins and the cereal flakes.

2. Coat a baking sheet with nonstick cooking spray. Drop rounded teaspoonfuls of dough onto the sheet, placing them 1-1/2 inches apart. Slightly flatten each cookie with the tip of a spoon.

3. Bake at 350°F for about 9 minutes, or until golden brown. Cool the cookies on the pan for 1 minute. Then transfer the cookies to wire racks, and cool completely. Serve immediately, or transfer to an airtight container and arrange in single layers separated by sheets of waxed paper.

COLOSSAL CHOCOLATE CHIPPERS

Yield: 30 cookies

NUTRITIONAL FACTS
(PER COOKIE)

CALORIES: 49

FAT: 0.7 G

PROTEIN: 0.7 G

CHOLESTEROL: 0 MG

SODIUM: 21 MG

FIBER: 0.5 G

CALCIUM: 2 MG

POTASSIUM: 25 MG

IRON: 0.3 MG

3/4 cup whole wheat flour

1/2 cup unbleached flour

2/3 cup sugar

3/4 teaspoon baking soda

1/4 cup Prune Purée (page 143)

2 tablespoons honey

1 teaspoon vanilla extract

1/3 cup chocolate chips

1/3 cup chopped walnuts (optional)

1 Combine the flours, sugar, and baking soda, and stir to mix well. Add the Prune Purée, honey, and vanilla extract, and stir to mix well. (If the dough seems crumbly, keep stirring until it holds together.) Stir in the chocolate chips and nuts if desired.

2 Coat a baking sheet with nonstick cooking spray. Drop slightly rounded teaspoonfuls of dough onto the sheet, placing them 1-1/2 inches apart. Slightly flatten each cookie with the tip of a spoon.

3 Bake at 350°F for about 9 minutes, or until golden brown. Cool the cookies on the pan for 1 minute. Then transfer the cookies to wire racks, and cool completely. Serve immediately, or transfer to an airtight container and arrange in single layers separated by sheets of waxed paper.

MINT CHOCOLATE DROPS

Yield: 30 cookies

NUTRITIONAL FACTS
(PER COOKIE)

CALORIES: 43

FAT: 0.8 G

PROTEIN: 0.8 G

CHOLESTEROL: 0 MG

SODIUM: 25 MG

FIBER: 0.8 G

CALCIUM: 3 MG

POTASSIUM: 34 MG

IRON: 0.3 MG

1 cup plus 1 tablespoon whole wheat flour

2 tablespoons cocoa powder

1/2 cup sugar

3/4 teaspoon baking soda

1/4 cup Prune Purée (page 143)

3 tablespoons chocolate syrup

1 teaspoon vanilla extract

1/3 cup mint chocolate chips

1. Combine the flour, cocoa, sugar, and baking soda, and stir to mix well. Add the Prune Purée, chocolate syrup, and vanilla extract, and stir to mix well. (If the dough seems crumbly, keep stirring until it holds together.) Stir in the chocolate chips.

2. Coat a baking sheet with nonstick cooking spray. Drop rounded teaspoonfuls of dough onto the sheet, placing them 1-1/2 inches apart. Slightly flatten each cookie with the tip of a spoon.

3. Bake at 350°F for about 10 minutes, or until golden brown. Cool the cookies on the pan for 1 minute. Then transfer the cookies to wire racks, and cool completely. Serve immediately, or transfer to an airtight container and arrange in single layers separated by sheets of waxed paper.

CARROT RAISIN COOKIES

Yield: 32 cookies

NUTRITIONAL FACTS
(PER COOKIE)

CALORIES: 48	
FAT: 0.3 G	
PROTEIN: 1.2 G	
CHOLESTEROL: 0 MG	
SODIUM: 27 MG	
FIBER: 1.2 G	
CALCIUM: 6 MG	
POTASSIUM: 64 MG	
IRON: 0.4 MG	

1-1/4 cups whole wheat flour
1 cup quick-cooking oats
1 teaspoon baking soda
1/2 teaspoon ground cinnamon
1/4 cup Prune Butter (page 143)
1/4 cup plus 2 tablespoons honey
3/4 cup finely grated carrots
1/3 cup golden raisins
32 pecan halves (optional)

1 Combine the flour, oats, baking soda, and cinnamon, and stir to mix well. Add the Prune Butter, honey, and carrots, and stir to mix well. Stir in the raisins.

2 Coat a baking sheet with nonstick cooking spray. Roll the dough into 1-inch balls, and place 1-1/2 inches apart on the sheet. (If the dough is too sticky to handle, place it in the freezer for a few minutes.) Using the bottom of a glass dipped in sugar, flatten the cookies to 1/4-inch thickness. As an alternative, press a pecan half in the center of each cookie to flatten the dough.

3 Bake at 275°F for about 18 minutes, or until golden brown. Cool the cookies on the pan for 1 minute. Then transfer the cookies to wire racks, and cool completely. Serve immediately, or transfer to an airtight container and arrange in single layers separated by sheets of waxed paper.

6

SQUASHING FAT

Squashes make great additions to baked goods. Rich in beta-carotene and fiber, these versatile vegetables moisten cakes, muffins, quick breads, and other sweet treats, and impart a lovely golden color as well. Use canned or cooked mashed pumpkin or butternut squash in these recipes. Cooked mashed sweet potatoes may also be used.

Some of these vegetables work better than others in certain recipes. Pumpkin, of course, is a natural fat substitute in pumpkin breads, muffins, and cakes. All you need do is increase the amount of pumpkin as you eliminate the fat. Mashed butternut squash and sweet potatoes add a velvety, super-moist texture to many baked goods, and are especially delicious in spice cakes and in cakes that feature pineapple, orange, or apple. Because the mild flavors of these fat substitutes do not overpower the taste of other ingredients, they can also be used in biscuits, scones, and plain muffins, and even in chocolate cakes and brownies.

GETTING THE FAT OUT

Below, you'll find some basic, simple-to-follow guidelines that will help you use squash and sweet potato to replace all or some of the fat in your own recipes. (For more helpful hints on modifying favorite recipes, see the inset on page 22.) After these guidelines, you'll find simple yet taste-tempting recipes that use these vegetables to eliminate the fat and enhance the flavor of a variety of homemade treats.

CAKE, MUFFIN, AND QUICK BREAD RECIPES

▓ Replace all or part of the butter, margarine, or other solid shortening in cake, muffin, and quick bread recipes with three-fourths as much cooked mashed pumpkin, butternut squash, or sweet potato. If oil is used, replace all or part of the oil with an equal amount of fat substitute. Mix up the batter. If it seems too dry, add a little more fat substitute. Some recipes may need a one-for-one substitution of squash for fat.

▓ When eliminating all of the fat from a recipe, reduce the number of eggs by half, or substitute 1 egg white for each whole egg in the recipe. In some recipes, you may be able to eliminate the eggs altogether by replacing each whole egg with 2 tablespoons of water or another liquid.

▓ To retain moistness, bake fat-free and fat-reduced cakes, muffins, and quick breads at a slightly lower-than-standard temperature. Bake muffins at 350°F. Bake quick breads and cakes at 325°F to 350°F. *Be careful not to overbake.* Bake just until a wooden toothpick inserted in the center comes out clean.

BISCUIT AND SCONE RECIPES

▓ Replace all or part of the butter, margarine, or other solid shortening in biscuit and scone recipes with three-fourths as much cooked mashed pumpkin, butternut squash, or sweet potato. If the recipe calls for oil, replace all or part of the oil with an equal amount of fat substitute. Mix up the dough. If it seems too stiff, add more fat substitute.

- When eliminating all of the fat from a biscuit or scone ⟩ reduce the number of eggs by half, or substitute 1 egg white each whole egg.
- Bake fat-free biscuits and scones at 375°F.

BROWNIE RECIPES

- Replace all or part of the butter, margarine, or other solid shortening in brownie recipes with three-fourths as much cooked mashed pumpkin, butternut squash, or sweet potato. If the recipe calls for oil, replace all or part of the oil with an equal amount of fat substitute.
- When eliminating all of the fat from a brownie recipe, you may replace each whole egg with 3 tablespoons of fat-free egg substitute if desired. However, it is not necessary to reduce the number of eggs.
- Bake fat-free brownies at 325°F, and check for doneness a few minutes before the end of the usual baking time. Remove the brownies from the oven as soon as the edges are firm and the center is almost set.

COOKIE RECIPES

- Replace half of the butter, margarine, or other solid shortening in cookie recipes with half to three-fourths as much cooked mashed pumpkin, sweet potato, or butternut squash. For example, if the recipe calls for 1 cup of butter, use 1/2 cup (8 tablespoons) of butter and 4 to 6 tablespoons of your chosen fat substitute. If the recipe calls for oil, replace half of the oil with three-fourths as much fat substitute. (You can replace more than half the fat, but the cookies may take on a cakey texture. Cookies that contain a high proportion of oats or oat bran are the easiest to make fat-free.)
- When reducing the fat in a cookie recipe, you may replace each whole egg with 3 tablespoons of fat-free egg substitute if desired. However, it is not necessary to reduce the number of eggs.
- Bake reduced-fat and fat-free cookies at 275°F to 300°F.

PKIN PRALINE PECAN MUFFINS

ffins

1-3/4 cups whole wheat flour

1/2 cup oat bran

1/2 cup brown sugar

1 tablespoon baking powder

2/3 cup cooked mashed pumpkin

1 cup skim milk

2 egg whites

1 teaspoon vanilla extract

Topping:

1 tablespoon finely chopped pecans

1 tablespoon brown sugar

1 To make the topping, combine the pecans and brown sugar until crumbly. Set aside.

2 Combine the flour, oat bran, brown sugar, and baking powder, and stir to mix well. Add the remaining ingredients, and stir just until the dry ingredients are moistened.

3 Coat muffin cups with nonstick cooking spray, and fill 3/4 full with the batter. Sprinkle the topping over the batter. Bake at 350°F for 15 to 18 minutes, or just until a wooden toothpick inserted in the center of a muffin comes out clean.

4 Remove the muffin tin from the oven, and allow it to sit for 5 minutes before removing the muffins. Serve warm or at room temperature.

SWEET POTATO CORN MUFFINS

Yield: 12 muffins

NUTRITIONAL FACTS
(PER MUFFIN)

CALORIES: 122

FAT: 0.5 G

PROTEIN: 3.3 G

CHOLESTEROL: 0 MG

SODIUM: 104 MG

FIBER: 2.8 G

CALCIUM: 43 MG

POTASSIUM: 255 MG

IRON: 1.4 MG

1-1/4 cups whole wheat flour

1/2 cup plus 2 tablespoons whole grain cornmeal

1 tablespoon baking powder

1/2 cup cooked mashed sweet potato

3/4 cup orange or apple juice

1/4 cup plus 2 tablespoons molasses

2 egg whites

1/3 cup dark raisins or chopped dates

1 Combine the flour, cornmeal, and baking powder, and stir to mix well. Add the sweet potato, orange or apple juice, molasses, and egg whites, and stir just until the dry ingredients are moistened. Fold in the raisins or dates.

2 Coat muffin cups with nonstick cooking spray, and fill 3/4 full with the batter. Bake at 350°F for 15 to 18 minutes, or just until a wooden toothpick inserted in the center of a muffin comes out clean.

3 Remove the muffin tin from the oven, and allow it to sit for 5 minutes before removing the muffins. Serve warm or at room temperature.

CRANBERRY PUMPKIN BREAD

Yield: 16 slices

NUTRITIONAL FACTS
(PER SLICE)

CALORIES: 100	
FAT: 0.3 G	
PROTEIN: 2.2 G	
CHOLESTEROL: 0 MG	
SODIUM: 78 MG	
FIBER: 2.5 G	
CALCIUM: 18 MG	
POTASSIUM: 110 MG	
IRON: 1 MG	

2 cups whole wheat flour

1/3 cup light brown sugar

1 teaspoon baking soda

1 teaspoon baking powder

1 teaspoon pumpkin pie spice

1 cup whole berry cranberry sauce

3/4 cup cooked mashed pumpkin

1/4 cup apple or orange juice

1 Combine the flour, sugar, baking soda, baking powder, and pumpkin pie spice, and stir to mix well. Add the remaining ingredients, and stir just until the dry ingredients are moistened.

2 Coat an 8-x-4-inch loaf pan with nonstick cooking spray. Spread the mixture evenly in the pan, and bake at 350°F for about 50 minutes, or just until a wooden toothpick inserted in the center of the loaf comes out clean.

3 Remove the bread from the oven, and let sit for 10 minutes. Invert the loaf onto a wire rack, turn right side up, and cool before slicing and serving.

PUMPKIN GINGERBREAD

Yield: 32 slices

NUTRITIONAL FACTS
(PER SLICE)

CALORIES: 63	
FAT: 0.3 G	
PROTEIN: 1.4 G	
CHOLESTEROL: 0 MG	
SODIUM: 29 MG	
FIBER: 1.5 G	
CALCIUM: 18 MG	
POTASSIUM: 137 MG	
IRON: 0.9 MG	

2 cups whole wheat flour

1 cup whole grain cornmeal

1 teaspoon baking soda

2 teaspoons ground ginger

1 teaspoon ground allspice

1 cup cooked mashed pumpkin

1-1/4 cups apple or orange juice

3/4 cup molasses

3/4 cup dark raisins (optional)

1. Combine the flour, cornmeal, baking soda, ginger, and allspice, and stir to mix well. Add the pumpkin, apple or orange juice, and molasses, and stir just until the dry ingredients are moistened. Fold in the raisins if desired.

2. Coat 4 one-pound cans with nonstick cooking spray. Divide the batter among the cans, and bake at 300°F for 40 to 45 minutes, or just until a wooden toothpick inserted in the center of a loaf comes out clean.

3. Remove the bread from the oven, and let sit for 10 minutes. Invert the loaves onto a wire rack, turn right side up, and cool before slicing and serving.

PUMPKIN PINEAPPLE BREAD

Yield: 16 slices

NUTRITIONAL FACTS
(PER SLICE)

CALORIES: 91

FAT: 0.5 G

PROTEIN: 2.4 G

CHOLESTEROL: 0 MG

SODIUM: 73 MG

FIBER: 2.3 G

CALCIUM: 15 MG

POTASSIUM: 108 MG

IRON: 0.9 MG

1-1/2 cups whole wheat flour

3/4 cup quick-cooking oats

1/2 cup sugar

1 teaspoon baking soda

1 teaspoon baking powder

1-1/2 teaspoons pumpkin pie spice

1 can (8 ounces) crushed pineapple
    packed in juice, undrained

1 cup cooked mashed pumpkin

1/3 cup chopped pecans (optional)

1 Combine the flour, oats, sugar, baking soda, baking powder, and pumpkin pie spice, and stir to mix well. Add the pineapple, including the juice, and the pumpkin, and stir just until the dry ingredients are moistened. Fold in the nuts if desired.

2 Coat an 8-x-4-inch loaf pan with nonstick cooking spray. Spread the batter evenly in the pan, and bake at 350°F for 45 to 50 minutes, or just until a wooden toothpick inserted in the center of the loaf comes out clean.

3 Remove the bread from the oven, and let sit for 10 minutes. Invert the loaf onto a wire rack, turn right side up, and cool before slicing and serving.

GOLDEN FRUITCAKE

Yield: 20 slices

1 cup plus 2 tablespoons whole wheat flour

1/2 teaspoon baking powder

1/2 cup plus 2 tablespoons nonfat
   buttermilk

1/4 cup cooked mashed pumpkin

2 tablespoons honey

2 egg whites

1/2 teaspoon vanilla extract

2/3 cup whole dried apricots

2/3 cup dried pineapple chunks

2/3 cup dried peach halves, cut in half

1/2 cup golden raisins

1/2 cup pecan halves (optional)

1 Combine the flour and baking powder, and stir to mix well. Add the buttermilk, pumpkin, honey, egg whites, and vanilla extract, and stir to mix well. Fold in the dried fruits and the nuts if desired.

2 Coat two 5-3/4-x-3-inch loaf pans with nonstick cooking spray. Divide the batter evenly between the pans, and bake at 325°F for about 45 minutes, or just until a wooden toothpick inserted in the center of a loaf comes out clean.

3 Remove the bread from the oven, and let sit for 10 minutes. Invert the loaves onto a wire rack, turn right side up, and cool to room temperature. Wrap in foil and let sit overnight before slicing and serving.

NUTTY NUTRITION

t's true—nuts *are* high in fat. In fact, one cup of nuts contains about 800 calories and 70 grams of fat. Does this mean that you should never eat nuts again? Definitely not. Everyone needs some fat to maintain good health, and nuts provide the essential fats we need in their most wholesome, unprocessed form. The fat in nuts is mostly unsaturated, and does not raise blood cholesterol levels. In fact, some studies show that people who eat nuts on a regular basis lower their risk of heart disease. If you need another reason to eat nuts, keep in mind that they also provide important minerals like magnesium, zinc, and copper, and are a good source of vitamin E, an antioxidant.

Because of their nutritional value, their crunch, and their great taste, nuts are included in many recipes in this book, and are optional ingredients in many more. If you like them, by all means use them. In fat-free recipes like these, you can afford to. Added in moderation to a recipe—say, 1/4 to 1/3 cup of nuts in a pan of brownies—nuts will not blow your fat budget.

Experiment with different kinds of nuts. Most people are familiar with walnuts, pecans, almonds, filberts, and peanuts. For a change of pace, try chopped Brazil nuts—the richest known source of the antioxidant mineral selenium. Or try pine nuts, an ingredient used in many traditional Italian baked goods.

Sunflower seeds, sesame seeds, flax seeds, and pumpkin seeds also make nutritious additions to cakes, cookies, muffins, and breads. Like nuts, these crunchy ingredients provide a variety of minerals, as well as vitamin E. Try them when you're in the mood for a different flavor and texture.

Top: Sweet Potato Corn Muffins (page 179)
Bottom: Cranberry Pumpkin Bread (page 180)

Top Left: Low-Fat Pound Cake (page 206)
Top Right: Almond Biscotti (page 220)
Bottom: Great Granola Cookies (page 223)

For nutty nutrition with half the fat, use toasted wheat germ in your baked goods. Wheat germ is an exceptional source of vitamin E and a number of minerals, and adds a slightly sweet nutlike taste to cookies, muffins, quick breads, and other treats. Add it to the batter, or sprinkle it on top for added crunch.

To bring out the flavor of both nuts and seeds, try toasting them. Toasting intensifies the flavors of nuts and seeds so much that you can often halve the amount used. Simply arrange the seeds or nuts in a single layer on a baking sheet, and bake at 350°F for about 10 minutes, or until lightly browned with a toasted, nutty smell. To save time, toast a large batch and store the extras in an airtight container in the refrigerator. That way, you'll always have a ready supply for all your baking adventures.

PUMPKIN DROP BISCUITS

Yield: 12 biscuits

NUTRITIONAL FACTS
(PER BISCUIT)

CALORIES: 93	
FAT: 0.4 G	
PROTEIN: 3.2 G	
CHOLESTEROL: 0 MG	
SODIUM: 112 MG	
FIBER: 1.7 G	
CALCIUM: 51 MG	
POTASSIUM: 105 MG	
IRON: 1 MG	

1 cup whole wheat flour

1 cup unbleached flour

2 tablespoons sugar

4 teaspoons baking powder

1/2 cup cooked mashed pumpkin

1 cup nonfat buttermilk

1 Combine the flours, sugar, and baking powder, and stir to mix well. In a separate bowl, combine the pumpkin and buttermilk, and stir until blended. Add the pumpkin mixture to the flour mixture, and stir just until the dry ingredients are moistened.

2 Coat a baking sheet with nonstick cooking spray. Drop heaping tablespoonfuls of dough onto the sheet, placing the biscuits 1/2 inch apart for soft biscuits, or 1-1/2 inches apart for crusty biscuits.

3 Bake at 375°F for about 18 minutes, or until lightly browned. Transfer to a serving plate, and serve hot.

BUTTERNUT OAT BRAN BISCUITS

Yield: 12 biscuits

NUTRITIONAL FACTS
(PER BISCUIT)

CALORIES: 109

FAT: 0.8 G

PROTEIN: 4.2 G

CHOLESTEROL: 0 MG

SODIUM: 107 MG

FIBER: 2.1 G

CALCIUM: 52 MG

POTASSIUM: 123 MG

IRON: 1.4 MG

1-3/4 cups plus 2 tablespoons unbleached flour

1 cup oat bran

1 tablespoon plus 1-1/2 teaspoons sugar

1 tablespoon baking powder

1/4 teaspoon baking soda

1/4 cup plus 2 tablespoons cooked mashed butternut squash or pumpkin

1 cup plus 2 tablespoons nonfat buttermilk

1 Combine the flour, oat bran, sugar, baking powder, and baking soda, and stir to mix well. In a separate bowl, combine the squash or pumpkin and the buttermilk, and stir until blended. Add the squash mixture to the flour mixture, and stir just until the dough leaves the sides of the bowl and rounds into a ball.

2 Turn the dough onto a floured surface, and pat into a 1/2-inch-thick sheet. Use a 2-1/2-inch glass or biscuit cutter to cut out 12 biscuits, dipping the rim of the glass in flour to prevent sticking. Reroll the scraps as needed.

3 Coat a baking sheet with nonstick cooking spray. Arrange the biscuits on the baking sheet, placing them 1/2 inch apart for soft biscuits, or 1-1/2 inches apart for crusty biscuits.

4 Bake at 375°F for 18 minutes, or until lightly browned. Transfer to a serving plate, and serve hot.

ʙUTTERSCOTCH BUNDT CAKE

Yield: 16 servings

NUTRITIONAL FACTS
(PER SERVING)

CALORIES: 180

FAT: 1.1 G

PROTEIN: 3.7 G

CHOLESTEROL: 0 MG

SODIUM: 98 MG

FIBER: 1.4 G

CALCIUM: 53 MG

POTASSIUM: 163 MG

IRON: 1.8 MG

2-1/3 cups unbleached flour

2/3 cup oat bran

1-1/3 cups light brown sugar

1 tablespoon plus
    1-1/2 teaspoons lecithin granules*

1-1/4 teaspoons baking soda

1-1/4 cups nonfat buttermilk

1/2 cup cooked mashed butternut squash
    or pumpkin

2 egg whites

2 tablespoons honey

2 teaspoons vanilla extract

Glaze:

1/3 cup confectioners' sugar

2 teaspoons light brown sugar

2 teaspoons skim milk

1   Combine the flour, oat bran, brown sugar, lecithin, and baking soda, and stir to mix well, pressing out any lumps with the back of a spoon. In a separate bowl, combine the buttermilk, squash or pumpkin, egg whites, honey, and vanilla extract. Add the buttermilk mixture to the flour mixture, and stir just enough to mix well.

2   Coat a 12-cup bundt pan with nonstick cooking spray. Spread the batter evenly in the pan, and bake at 350°F for about 40 minutes, or just until a wooden toothpick inserted in the center of the cake comes out clean.

3   Cool the cake in the pan for 20 minutes. Then invert onto a wire rack, and cool to room temperature. Transfer to a serving plate.

4 To make the glaze, combine the confectioners' sugar, brown sugar, and milk until smooth. Drizzle the glaze over the cake, and let sit for at least 15 minutes before slicing and serving.

* For information on lecithin, see the inset on page 83.

SWEET POTATO SNACK CAKE

Yield: 8 servings

NUTRITIONAL FACTS (PER SERVING)
CALORIES: 183
FAT: 0.4 G
PROTEIN: 4 G
CHOLESTEROL: 0 MG
SODIUM: 141 MG
FIBER: 2.9 G
CALCIUM: 57 MG
POTASSIUM: 252 MG
IRON: 1.9 MG

1 cup whole wheat flour
3/4 cup light brown sugar
2 teaspoons baking powder
1/2 teaspoon ground cinnamon
1/8 teaspoon ground nutmeg
1-1/2 cups cooked mashed sweet potato
2 egg whites
2 tablespoons skim milk
2 tablespoons confectioners' sugar (optional)

1 Combine the flour, brown sugar, baking powder, and spices, and stir to mix well. Add the remaining ingredients, and stir to mix well.

2 Coat an 8-inch square pan with nonstick cooking spray. Spread the batter evenly in the pan, and bake at 325°F for 40 to 45 minutes, or just until a wooden toothpick inserted in the center of the cake comes out clean.

3 Cool the cake to room temperature. Sift the confectioners' sugar over the cake if desired, cut into squares, and serve.

ORANGE CRUMB CAKE

Yield: 8 servings

3/4 cup unbleached flour

1/2 cup whole wheat flour

1/2 cup sugar

1 teaspoon baking powder

1/4 teaspoon baking soda

1/2 cup orange juice

1/4 cup cooked mashed pumpkin or butternut squash

3 tablespoons fat-free egg substitute

1 teaspoon vanilla extract

Crumb Topping:

1/4 cup plus 2 tablespoons quick-cooking oats

2 tablespoons toasted wheat germ or finely chopped pecans

1 tablespoon light brown sugar

1 tablespoon frozen orange juice concentrate, thawed

Glaze:

1/4 cup confectioners' sugar

2 teaspoons frozen orange juice concentrate, thawed

1 To make the topping, stir the topping ingredients together until moist and crumbly. Set aside.

2 Combine the flours, sugar, baking powder, and baking soda, and stir to mix well. Add the orange juice, pumpkin or butternut squash, egg substitute, and vanilla extract, and stir to mix well.

3 Coat an 8-inch round pan with nonstick cooking spray. Spread the batter evenly in the pan, and sprinkle the topping over the batter.

4 Bake at 350°F for 25 minutes, or just until a wooden toothpick inserted in the center of the cake comes out clean. Cover loosely with aluminum foil during the last 5 minutes of baking if the topping starts to brown too quickly. Cool at room temperature for 5 minutes.

5 To make the glaze, combine the glaze ingredients until smooth. Drizzle the glaze over the cake, cut into wedges, and serve warm.

GEORGIA FUDGE BARS

Yield: 16 servings

NUTRITIONAL FACTS *(PER SERVING)*
CALORIES: 78
FAT: 0.5 G
PROTEIN: 1.7 G
CHOLESTEROL: 0 MG
SODIUM: 29 MG
FIBER: 1.1 G
CALCIUM: 6 MG
POTASSIUM: 51 MG
IRON: 0.5 MG

1/3 cup unbleached flour

1/3 cup oat bran

1/3 cup cocoa powder

1 cup sugar

1/8 teaspoon salt (optional)

1/2 cup cooked mashed sweet potato

3 egg whites

1 teaspoon vanilla extract

1/3 cup chopped pecans (optional)

1 Combine the flour, oat bran, cocoa, sugar, and salt, if desired, and stir to mix well. Add the sweet potato, egg whites, and vanilla extract, and stir to mix well. Fold in the nuts if desired.

2 Coat an 8-inch square pan with nonstick cooking spray. Spread the mixture evenly in the pan, and bake at 325°F for about 25 minutes, or until the edges are firm and the center is almost set.

3 Cool to room temperature, cut into squares, and serve.

SUPER-MOIST PINEAPPLE CAKE

Yield: 16 servings

NUTRITIONAL FACTS (PER SERVING)
CALORIES: 154
FAT: 0.2 G
PROTEIN: 2.3 G
CHOLESTEROL: 0 MG
SODIUM: 85 MG
FIBER: 0.9 G
CALCIUM: 10 MG
POTASSIUM: 53 MG
IRON: 1 MG

2 cups unbleached flour

1-1/2 cups sugar

1-1/2 teaspoons baking soda

1 cup cooked mashed pumpkin

1 can (8 ounces) crushed pineapple packed in juice, undrained

1/2 cup pineapple or orange juice

1-1/2 teaspoons vanilla extract

3–4 tablespoons confectioners' sugar

1 Combine the flour, sugar, and baking soda, and stir to mix well. Stir in the pumpkin, the crushed pineapple, including the juice, and the pineapple or orange juice and vanilla extract.

2 Coat a 9-x-13-inch pan with nonstick cooking spray. Spread the batter evenly in the pan, and bake at 350°F for 35 minutes, or just until a wooden toothpick inserted in the center of the cake comes out clean.

3 Cool the cake to room temperature. Sift the confectioners' sugar over the cake, cut into squares, and serve.

PUMPKIN SPICE BARS

Yield: 32 servings

NUTRITIONAL FACTS
(PER SERVING)
CALORIES: 76
FAT: 0.7 G
PROTEIN: 1.6 G
CHOLESTEROL: 0 MG
SODIUM: 43 MG
FIBER: 0.9 G
CALCIUM: 17 MG
POTASSIUM: 118 MG
IRON: 0.9 MG

1-1/2 cups unbleached flour

1 cup whole wheat flour

1/2 cup sugar

1-1/2 teaspoons baking soda

1 teaspoon ground cinnamon

1 teaspoon ground cloves

1/4 teaspoon ground nutmeg

1/2 cup cooked mashed pumpkin

2/3 cup molasses

1 cup water

2 egg whites

1/2 cup golden raisins

1/4 cup chopped walnuts

1 Combine the flours, sugar, baking soda, and spices, and stir to mix well. Add the pumpkin, molasses, water, and egg whites, and stir to mix well. Fold in the raisins and nuts.

2 Coat a 9-x-13-inch pan with nonstick cooking spray. Spread the mixture evenly in the pan, and bake at 350°F for 30 to 35 minutes, or until a wooden toothpick inserted in the center comes out clean.

3 Cool to room temperature, cut into squares, and serve.

GREAT PUMPKIN COOKIES

Yield: 38 cookies

NUTRITIONAL FACTS
(PER COOKIE)
CALORIES: 45
FAT: 0.5 G
PROTEIN: 0.9 G
CHOLESTEROL: 0 MG
SODIUM: 18 MG
FIBER: 0.9 G
CALCIUM: 9 MG
POTASSIUM: 54 MG
IRON: 0.5 MG

1 cup whole wheat flour
1 cup oat bran
3/4 cup light brown sugar
3/4 teaspoon baking soda
1/2 cup cooked mashed pumpkin
1/4 cup maple syrup

Coating:

2 tablespoons finely ground pecans
2 tablespoons sugar

1 To make the coating, combine the ground pecans and 2 tablespoons of sugar in a small bowl, and stir to mix well. Set aside.

2 Combine the flour, oat bran, brown sugar, and baking soda, and stir to mix well. Stir in the pumpkin and maple syrup.

3 Coat a baking sheet with nonstick cooking spray. Roll the dough into 1-inch balls. (If the dough is too sticky to handle, place it in the freezer for a few minutes.) Roll each ball in the pecan mixture until coated, and place the balls 1-1/2 inches apart on the baking sheet. Use the bottom of a glass to flatten each cookie to 1/4-inch thickness.

4 Bake at 300°F for 15 minutes, or until lightly browned. Cool the cookies on the pan for 1 minute. Then transfer the cookies to wire racks, and cool completely. Serve immediately, or transfer to an airtight container and arrange in single layers separated by sheets of waxed paper.

7

BAKING WITH REDUCED-FAT MARGARINE & LIGHT BUTTER

Contrary to popular belief, you *can* bake with reduced-fat margarine and light butter. Replacing regular margarine and butter with reduced-fat versions can reduce the fat in baked goods by up to 55 percent without greatly altering taste and texture. This makes it possible to produce light and tender buttery-tasting cakes, crisp cookies, tender pie crusts, and flaky pastries—baked goods not easily made fat-free. The recipes in this chapter emphasize these types of treats, rather than muffins and other baked goods that can easily be made fat-free with the methods described in earlier chapters.

For baking, choose brands of butter and margarine that have 5 to 6 grams of fat and 50 calories per tablespoon. (Full-fat versions have 11 grams of fat and about 100 calories per tablespoon.) Margarines and butters with less fat than this do not'work well in baked goods.

GETTING THE FAT OUT

Because reduced-fat butter and margarine are diluted with water, they cannot be substituted one-for-one for the full-fat versions. Below, you'll find some basic guidelines that will help you use these products in your own recipes. (For more helpful hints on modifying recipes, see the inset on page 22.) After the guidelines, you'll find some tried-and-true recipes that use reduced-fat products to maintain the pleasing taste and texture and maximize the healthfulness of cakes, cookies, and other baked goods.

CAKE, MUFFIN, AND QUICK BREAD RECIPES

▓ Replace all of the butter, margarine, or other solid shortening in cake, muffin, and quick bread recipes with three-fourths as much reduced-fat margarine or light butter.

▓ When reducing the fat in a recipe, you may replace each whole egg with 3 tablespoons of fat-free egg substitute if desired. However, it is not necessary to reduce the number of eggs.

▓ Bake reduced-fat muffins at 350°F to 375°F. Bake quick breads and cakes at 350°F. Check for doneness a few minutes before the end of the usual baking time.

BISCUIT AND SCONE RECIPES

▓ Replace all of the butter, margarine, or other solid shortening in biscuit and scone recipes with three-fourths as much reduced-fat margarine or light butter.

▓ When reducing the fat in a recipe, you may replace each whole egg with 3 tablespoons of fat-free egg substitute if desired. However, it is not necessary to reduce the number of eggs.

▓ Bake reduced-fat biscuits and scones at 400°F just until lightly browned.

BROWNIE RECIPES

▓ Replace all of the butter, margarine, or other solid shortening in brownie recipes with three-fourths as much reduced-fat margarine or light butter.

▓ When reducing the fat in a recipe, you may replace each whole egg with 3 tablespoons of fat-free egg substitute if desired. However, it is not necessary to reduce the number of eggs.

■ Bake reduced-fat brownies at 325°F, and check for doneness a few minutes before the end of the usual baking time. Remove the brownies from the oven as soon as the edges are firm and the center is almost set.

COOKIE RECIPES

■ Replace all of the butter, margarine, or other solid shortening in cookie recipes with three-fourths as much reduced-fat margarine or light butter.

■ When reducing the fat in a recipe, you may replace each whole egg with 3 tablespoons of fat-free egg substitute if desired. However, it is not necessary to reduce the number of eggs.

■ Bake reduced-fat cookies at 300°F just until golden brown.

■ Use reduced-fat margarine and light butter only in cookie recipes that do not contain significant amounts of applesauce, buttermilk, mashed bananas, or other liquidy ingredients. Because reduced-fat margarine and butter are half water, they do contribute some liquid to the recipe. Too much liquid in cookies can create a cakey texture.

ROLLED PIE CRUST RECIPES

■ Replace all of the butter, margarine, or other solid shortening in rolled pie crust recipes with three-fourths as much reduced-fat margarine or light butter.

■ Bake reduced-fat pie crusts at 375°F to 400°F just until golden brown.

CRUMB CRUST RECIPES

■ Replace all of the butter, margarine, or other solid shortening in crumb crusts—graham cracker and cereal crusts, for instance—with three-fourths as much reduced-fat margarine or light butter.

■ Bake reduced-fat crumb crusts at 350°F just until lightly browned.

CRUMB TOPPING RECIPES

■ Replace all of the butter, margarine, or other solid shortening in crumb topping recipes with three-fourths as much reduced-fat margarine or light butter.

SUNDAY MORNING SCONES

Yield: 12 scones

NUTRITIONAL FACTS
(PER SCONE)

CALORIES: 97

FAT: 2 G

PROTEIN: 2.7 G

CHOLESTEROL: 0 MG

SODIUM: 142 MG

FIBER: 1.7 G

CALCIUM: 24 MG

POTASSIUM: 74 MG

IRON: 0.9 MG

1 cup whole wheat flour

1 cup unbleached flour

1/2 teaspoon baking soda

2 teaspoons baking powder

1/4 cup reduced-fat margarine or light butter

2/3 cup unsweetened applesauce

1/3 cup nonfat buttermilk

1/3 cup dark raisins (optional)

Skim milk

1 Combine the flours, baking soda, and baking powder, and stir to mix well. Use a pastry cutter to cut in the margarine or butter until the mixture resembles coarse meal. Stir in the applesauce and just enough of the buttermilk to form a stiff dough. Fold in the raisins if desired.

2 Form the dough into a ball, and turn onto a lightly floured surface. With floured hands, shape the dough into a 7-inch circle.

3 Coat a baking sheet with nonstick cooking spray. Place the dough on the sheet, and use a sharp floured knife to cut it into 12 wedges. Pull the wedges out slightly to leave a 1/2-inch space between them. Brush the tops lightly with skim milk.

4 Bake at 400°F for 16 to 18 minutes, or until lightly browned. Transfer to a serving plate, and serve hot.

LEMON-POPPY SEED POUND CAKE

Yield: 16 slices

NUTRITIONAL FACTS (PER SERVING)
CALORIES: 197
FAT: 3.6 G
PROTEIN: 4.3 G
CHOLESTEROL: 0 MG
SODIUM: 116 MG
FIBER: 1.3 G
CALCIUM: 51 MG
POTASSIUM: 100 MG
IRON: 1.2 MG

1/2 cup reduced-fat margarine or light butter

1-1/2 cups sugar

3 egg whites

2-1/3 cups unbleached flour

2/3 cup oat bran

1-1/2 tablespoons poppy seeds

1/2 teaspoon baking soda

1 cup nonfat lemon yogurt

3 tablespoons lemon juice

1 tablespoon freshly grated lemon rind, or 1 teaspoon dried

Glaze:

1/3 cup confectioners' sugar

2 teaspoons lemon juice

1. Combine the margarine or butter and the sugar in the bowl of an electric mixer, and beat until smooth. Add the egg whites, and beat until smooth. In a separate bowl, combine the flour, oat bran, poppy seeds, and baking soda. Add the flour mixture and the yogurt, lemon juice, and lemon rind to the margarine mixture, and beat just until well mixed.

2. Coat a 12-cup bundt pan with nonstick cooking spray. Spread the batter evenly in the pan, and bake at 350°F for 40 minutes, or just until a wooden toothpick inserted in the center of the cake comes out clean. Cool the cake in the pan for 20 minutes. Then invert onto a wire rack, and cool to room temperature.

3. To make the glaze, combine the confectioners' sugar and lemon juice, and stir until smooth. Transfer the cake to a serving platter, and drizzle the glaze over the cake. Let sit for at least 15 minutes before slicing and serving.

RASPBERRY RIPPLE CAKE

Yield: 16 servings

NUTRITIONAL FACTS
(PER SERVING)

CALORIES: 169

FAT: 2 G

PROTEIN: 3.3 G

CHOLESTEROL: 0 MG

SODIUM: 117 MG

FIBER: 1.6 G

CALCIUM: 29 MG

POTASSIUM: 83 MG

IRON: 1.1 MG

For variety, substitute blueberries for the raspberries.

3/4 cup fresh or frozen (thawed) raspberries

1 tablespoon sugar

1/4 cup reduced-fat margarine or light butter

1-1/4 cups sugar

3 egg whites

1 teaspoon almond extract

2-1/4 cups unbleached flour

3/4 cup oat bran

1-1/4 teaspoons baking soda

1-1/4 cups nonfat buttermilk

Glaze:

1/3 cup confectioners' sugar

1/4 teaspoon almond extract

2 teaspoons nonfat buttermilk

1 Place the raspberries and 1 tablespoon of sugar in a food processor or blender, and purée. Set aside.

2 Combine the margarine or butter and the sugar in the bowl of an electric mixer, and beat until smooth. Beat in the egg whites and almond extract until smooth. In a separate bowl, combine the flour, oat bran, and baking soda. Add the flour mixture and the buttermilk to the margarine mixture, and beat just until well mixed.

3 Remove 3/4 cup of the batter, and mix with the raspberry purée. Set aside.

4 Coat a 12-cup bundt pan with nonstick cooking spray. Spread 2/3 of the plain batter evenly in the pan. Top with the raspberry batter, and follow with the remaining plain batter.

5 Bake at 350°F for 35 to 40 minutes, or just until a wooden toothpick inserted in the center of the cake comes out clean. Cool the cake in the pan for 10 minutes. Then invert onto a wire rack, and cool to room temperature.

6 To make the glaze, combine the glaze ingredients and stir until smooth. Transfer the cake to a serving platter, and drizzle the glaze over the cake. Let sit for at least 15 minutes before slicing and serving.

BANANA CRUNCH CAKE

Yield: 10 servings

NUTRITIONAL FACTS
(PER SLICE)

CALORIES: 222

FAT: 3.8 G

PROTEIN: 4.6 G

CHOLESTEROL: 0 MG

SODIUM: 134 MG

FIBER: 2.2 G

CALCIUM: 30 MG

POTASSIUM: 191 MG

IRON: 1.5 MG

1 cup plus 2 tablespoons unbleached flour

1/2 cup whole wheat flour

1/2 cup sugar

2 teaspoons baking powder

1 cup mashed very ripe banana
  (about 2 large)

1/4 cup reduced-fat margarine or light
  butter, melted

2 egg whites

1 teaspoon vanilla extract

Topping:

3/4 cup quick-cooking oats

3 tablespoons brown sugar

2 tablespoons chopped walnuts

2 tablespoons maple syrup

Glaze:

1/4 cup confectioners' sugar

1-1/2 teaspoons skim milk

1 pinch ground cinnamon

1 To make the topping, combine the topping ingredients, and stir until moist and crumbly. Set aside.

2 Combine the flours, sugar, and baking powder, and stir to mix well. Add the banana, margarine or butter, egg whites, and vanilla extract, and stir just until mixed.

3 Coat a 9-inch round pan with nonstick cooking spray. Spread the batter evenly in the pan, and sprinkle the topping over the batter. Bake at 350°F for 30 minutes, or just until a wooden toothpick

inserted in the center of the cake comes out clean. Cool the cake at room temperature for 10 minutes.

4 To make the glaze, combine the confectioners' sugar, milk, and cinnamon, and stir until smooth. Drizzle the glaze over the cake, cut into wedges, and serve warm or at room temperature.

PEACH RAISIN CRISP

Yield: 6 servings

NUTRITIONAL FACTS (PER SERVING)
CALORIES: 190
FAT: 3.6 G
PROTEIN: 3.3 G
CHOLESTEROL: 0 MG
SODIUM: 73 MG
FIBER: 3.9 G
CALCIUM: 26 MG
POTASSIUM: 384 MG
IRON: 1.2 MG

Fruit Filling:

4 cups fresh or frozen (thawed) sliced peaches (about 5 medium)

1/4 cup plus 2 tablespoons dark raisins

Topping:

3/4 cup quick-cooking oats

3 tablespoons whole wheat flour

1/4 cup brown sugar

1/2 teaspoon ground cinnamon

3 tablespoons reduced-fat margarine or light butter, cut into pieces

1 To make the fruit filling, toss the peach slices with the raisins. Coat a 9-inch deep dish pie pan with nonstick cooking spray, and spread the fruit evenly in the pan.

2 To make topping, combine oats, flour, brown sugar, and cinnamon, and stir to mix well. Use a pastry cutter to cut margarine or butter into the oat mixture until crumbly. Sprinkle topping over the fruit.

3 Bake at 375°F for 30 to 35 minutes, or until the topping is golden brown. Serve warm with nonfat vanilla yogurt if desired.

OLD-FASHIONED STRAWBERRY SHORTCAKE

Yield: 10 servings

NUTRITIONAL FACTS
(PER SERVING)

CALORIES: 198

FAT: 3.8 G

PROTEIN: 4.9 G

CHOLESTEROL: 0 MG

SODIUM: 186 MG

FIBER: 3.6 G

CALCIUM: 79 MG

POTASSIUM: 255 MG

IRON: 1.6 MG

Biscuits:

1-1/2 cups unbleached flour

1/2 cup oat bran

1/4 cup sugar

1 tablespoon baking powder

4 tablespoons chilled reduced-fat margarine or light butter, cut into pieces

2/3 cup nonfat buttermilk

3 tablespoons fat-free egg substitute

Fruit Topping:

3 cups sliced fresh strawberries

1/3 cup sugar

Cream Topping:

1/2 cup nonfat vanilla yogurt

3/4 cup light whipped topping

1 To make the fruit topping, combine the strawberries and sugar. Cover and refrigerate for several hours or overnight to allow the juices to develop.

2 To make the cream topping, gently fold the yogurt into the whipped topping. Chill until ready to serve.

3 Combine the flour, oat bran, sugar, and baking powder, and stir to mix well. Use a pastry cutter to cut in the margarine or butter until the mixture resembles coarse crumbs. In a separate bowl, combine the buttermilk and egg substitute. Add to the flour mixture, and stir just until moistened.

4 Coat a baking sheet with nonstick cooking spray. Drop heaping table-spoonfuls of the batter onto the sheet to make 10 biscuits. (Place 3/4 inches apart for soft biscuits, or 2 inches apart for crusty biscuits.)

5 Bake at 400°F for 18 to 20 minutes, or until lightly browned. Remove from the oven, and let sit for at least 5 minutes. (The biscuits may be served warm or at room temperature.)

6 To assemble the shortcakes, slice each biscuit in half lengthwise. Place the bottom half of each biscuit on an individual serving plate, and top with 3 tablespoons of the strawberry topping. Add the top half of the biscuit and another 3 tablespoons of strawberries. Drop a heaping tablespoonful of the cream topping over the strawberries, and serve.

LOW-FAT POUND CAKE

Yield: 16 slices

NUTRITIONAL FACTS
(PER SLICE)

CALORIES: 141

FAT: 2.0 G

PROTEIN: 3.3 G

CHOLESTEROL: 0 MG

SODIUM: 90 MG

FIBER: 0.9 G

CALCIUM: 33 MG

POTASSIUM: 77 MG

IRON: 0.8 MG

5 tablespoons reduced-fat margarine or
  light butter

1-1/4 cups sugar

3 egg whites

1-1/2 teaspoons vanilla extract

1-2/3 cups unbleached flour

1/2 cup oat bran

1/2 teaspoon baking soda

1 cup vanilla or lemon nonfat yogurt

1 Combine the margarine or butter and the sugar in the bowl of an electric mixer, and beat until smooth. Add the egg whites and vanilla extract, and beat until smooth. In a separate bowl, combine the flour, oat bran, and baking soda. Add the flour mixture and the yogurt to the margarine mixture, and beat just enough to mix well.

2 Coat an 8-x-4-inch loaf pan with nonstick cooking spray. Spread the mixture evenly in the pan, and bake at 350°F for 55 to 60 minutes, or just until a wooden toothpick inserted in the center of the loaf comes out clean.

3 Remove the cake from the oven, and let sit for 20 minutes. Invert the cake onto a wire rack, turn right side up, and cool to room temperature before slicing and serving.

MINI CHERRY COBBLERS

Yield: 6 servings

Filling:

4 cups pitted fresh or frozen (thawed) sweet cherries

3 tablespoons sugar

1 tablespoon frozen apple juice concentrate, thawed

4 teaspoons cornstarch

Crust:

1/2 cup unbleached flour

1/3 cup whole wheat flour

1 tablespoon sugar

3 tablespoons chilled reduced-fat margarine or light butter, cut into pieces

2 tablespoons plus 1 teaspoon skim milk

1 egg white, beaten

Sugar (optional)

1. To make the filling, combine the filling ingredients and toss to mix well. Coat six 6-ounce custard cups with nonstick cooking spray, and divide the mixture evenly among the cups. Set aside.

2. To make the crust, combine the flours and sugar, and stir to mix well. Use a pastry cutter to cut in the margarine or butter until the mixture resembles coarse crumbs. Add the milk, and stir just until moistened.

3. Divide the dough into 6 pieces, and shape each piece into a ball. One at a time, place each ball on a lightly floured surface, and roll into a 4-inch circle. Place each crust over a filled custard cup, and pinch the dough to form a decorative edging. Brush the tops lightly with egg white, and sprinkle with sugar if desired. Using a sharp knife, cut 4 slits in the center of each crust to allow the steam to escape.

4. Place the cups on a baking sheet, and bake at 375°F for 30 minutes, or until the filling is bubbly and the crust is golden brown. Serve warm.

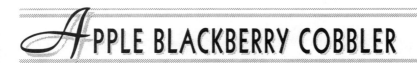

APPLE BLACKBERRY COBBLER

Yield: 8 servings

NUTRITIONAL FACTS
(PER SERVING)

CALORIES: 164

FAT: 2.9 G

PROTEIN: 2.2 G

CHOLESTEROL: 0 MG

SODIUM: 75 MG

FIBER: 4.4 G

CALCIUM: 29 MG

POTASSIUM: 214 MG

IRON: 1.2 MG

Fruit Filling:

6 cups sliced peeled fresh apples (about 7 medium)

1-1/2 cups fresh or frozen (thawed) blackberries

1/3 cup light brown sugar

1-1/2 tablespoons cornstarch

1 tablespoon frozen apple juice concentrate, thawed

Crust:

1/2 cup oat bran

1/2 cup unbleached flour

1/2 teaspoon baking powder

3 tablespoons chilled reduced-fat margarine or light butter, cut into pieces

2–3 tablespoons cold water

Glaze:

2 teaspoons beaten egg white

2 teaspoons water

1 tablespoon sugar

1 To make the fruit filling, combine all of the filling ingredients, and toss to mix well. Coat a 10-inch pie pan with nonstick cooking spray, and spread the fruit evenly in the pan.

2 To make the crust, combine the oat bran, flour, and baking powder, and stir to mix well. Use a pastry cutter to cut the margarine or butter into the flour mixture until the mixture resembles coarse crumbs. Stir in just enough of the water to make a stiff dough that leaves the sides of the bowl and forms a ball.

3 Turn the dough onto a generously floured surface, and roll into an 11-inch circle. Use a knife or pizza wheel to cut the circle into 1/2-inch strips. Lay half of the crust strips over the filling, spacing the strips 1/2

inch apart. Lay the remaining strips over the filling in the opposite direction to form a lattice top. Trim the edges to make the dough conform to the shape of the pan.

4 Combine the egg white and water, and brush over the crust. Sprinkle the sugar over the egg white mixture. Bake at 375°F for 45 minutes, or until the filling is bubbly and the crust is lightly browned. Cool for at least 15 minutes, and serve warm or at room temperature.

COCONUT OAT PIE CRUST

Yield: One 9-inch pie crust for 8 servings

NUTRITIONAL FACTS
(PER SERVING)
CALORIES: 91
FAT: 3.5 G
PROTEIN: 2.2 G
CHOLESTEROL: 0 MG
SODIUM: 53 MG
FIBER: 1.7 G
CALCIUM: 11 MG
POTASSIUM: 71 MG
IRON: 0.7 MG

1 cup quick-cooking oats

1/4 cup whole wheat flour

2 tablespoons light brown sugar

2 tablespoons finely grated coconut

3 tablespoons melted reduced-fat margarine or light butter

1/2 teaspoon coconut-flavored extract

1 Combine the oats, flour, brown sugar, and coconut, and stir to mix well. Add the margarine or butter and the coconut extract, and stir until the mixture is moist and crumbly.

2 Coat a 9-inch pie pan with nonstick cooking spray. Use the back of a spoon to press the crumbs against the sides and bottom of the pan, forming an even crust. Periodically dip the spoon in sugar to prevent sticking.

3 Bake the pie shell at 350°F for 18 minutes, or until golden brown around the edges. Cool the crust to room temperature, and fill as desired.

HONEY GRAHAM PIE CRUST

Yield: One 9-inch pie crust for 8 servings

NUTRITIONAL FACTS
(PER SERVING)

CALORIES: 93	
FAT: 1.1 G	
PROTEIN: 1.5 G	
CHOLESTEROL: 0 MG	
SODIUM: 152 MG	
FIBER: 0.5 G	
CALCIUM: 8 MG	
POTASSIUM: 75 MG	
IRON: 0.7 MG	

If you can't find fat-free graham crackers, use regular graham crackers, which are quite low in fat.

8 large (2-1/2-x-5-inch) fat-free graham crackers

1-1/2 tablespoons reduced-fat margarine or light butter, cut into pieces

1-1/2 tablespoons honey

1 Break the crackers in pieces, and place in the bowl of a food processor or in a blender. Process into fine crumbs. Measure the crumbs. There should be 1-1/4 cups.

2 Return the crumbs to the food processor, and add the margarine or butter and the honey. Process until moist and crumbly.

3 Coat a 9-inch pie pan with nonstick cooking spray. Use the back of a spoon to press the crumbs against the sides and bottom of the pan, forming an even crust. Periodically dip the spoon in sugar to prevent sticking.

4 Bake the pie shell at 350°F for 10 minutes, or until the edges feel firm and dry. Cool the crust to room temperature, and fill as desired.

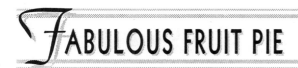ABULOUS FRUIT PIE

Yield: 8 servings

NUTRITIONAL FACTS
(PER SERVING)

CALORIES: 174

FAT: 3.9 G

PROTEIN: 3 G

CHOLESTEROL: 0 MG

SODIUM: 55 MG

FIBER: 3.5 G

CALCIUM: 26 MG

POTASSIUM: 318 MG

IRON: 1.1 MG

1 prepared Coconut Oat Pie Crust
(page 209)

Filling:

1 cup sliced fresh strawberries

2 kiwi fruit, peeled and sliced
1/4 inch thick

1 cup sliced bananas

5 strawberry slices

Pineapple Glaze:

2-1/2 tablespoons cornstarch

2 tablespoons sugar

3/4 cup orange juice

1 can (8 ounces) crushed pineapple
packed in juice, undrained

1 To make the glaze, combine the cornstarch and sugar in a medium-sized saucepan, and stir to mix well. Slowly stir in first the orange juice and then the crushed pineapple, including the juice. Place over medium-low heat and cook, stirring constantly, until the glaze mixture is thickened and bubbly. Remove the saucepan from the heat, and set aside for 15 minutes.

2 Spread half of the pineapple glaze evenly over the bottom of the pie crust. Arrange the strawberries in a circular pattern over the pineapple mixture. Arrange the kiwi slices over the strawberries. Arrange the banana slices over the kiwi. Top with the remaining glaze, and garnish with the strawberry slices.

3 Chill the pie for several hours, or until the glaze is set. Cut into wedges and serve cold.

STRAWBERRY SWIRL CHEESECAKE

Yield: 10 servings

NUTRITIONAL FACTS
(PER SERVING)

CALORIES: 239

FAT: 1 G

PROTEIN: 15 G

CHOLESTEROL: 0 MG

SODIUM: 243 MG

FIBER: 0.6 G

CALCIUM: 479 MG

POTASSIUM: 72 MG

IRON: 1 MG

1 recipe Honey Graham Pie Crust (page 210)

2/3 cup low-sugar strawberry preserves

2 containers (15 ounces each) nonfat ricotta cheese

1/2 cup nonfat sour cream or plain nonfat yogurt

3/4 cup fat-free egg substitute or 6 egg whites

2/3 cup sugar

1/4 cup unbleached flour

2 teaspoons vanilla extract

1 Coat a 9-inch springform pan with nonstick cooking spray. Prepare the graham cracker crust as directed, but pat it over the bottom of the pan and 1/2 inch up the sides. Bake at 350°F for 8 minutes, or until the edges are firm and dry and lightly browned. Set aside to cool.

2 If using a microwave oven, place the jam in a microwave-safe bowl, and microwave uncovered at 50-percent power for 2 minutes or until runny. If using a conventional stove top, place the jam in a small saucepan over low heat and cook, stirring constantly, until runny. Set aside.

3 Place the ricotta, sour cream or yogurt, and egg substitute in the bowl of a food processor or in a blender, and process until smooth. Add the sugar, flour, and vanilla extract, and process until smooth.

4 Spread half of the cheese filling evenly over the graham cracker crust. Spoon half of the heated jam randomly over the filling. Top with the remaining filling. Then spoon the rest of the jam randomly over the top. Draw a knife through the batter to produce a marbled effect.

5 Bake at 350°F for 60 to 70 minutes, or until the center is set. Turn the oven off, and allow the cake to cool in the oven with the door ajar for 30 minutes.

6 Chill the cake for at least 8 hours. Remove the collar of the pan just before slicing and serving.

CARROT RAISIN BARS

Yield: 16 servings

NUTRITIONAL FACTS (PER SERVING)
CALORIES: 108
FAT: 1.6 G
PROTEIN: 2.4 G
CHOLESTEROL: 0 MG
SODIUM: 57 MG
FIBER: 1.9 G
CALCIUM: 22 MG
POTASSIUM: 159 MG
IRON: 1 MG

3 tablespoons reduced-fat margarine or light butter
3/4 cup brown sugar
1 egg white
1 teaspoon vanilla extract
3/4 cup whole wheat flour
3/4 cup quick-cooking oats
1/4 cup toasted wheat germ
1 teaspoon ground cinnamon
1 teaspoon baking powder
1-1/4 cups grated carrots (about 2-1/2 medium)
1/2 cup golden raisins

1 Combine the margarine or butter and brown sugar in the bowl of a food processor or electric mixer, and process until smooth. Add the egg white and vanilla extract, and process until smooth.

2 In a separate bowl, combine the flour, oats, wheat germ, cinnamon, and baking powder. Add the flour mixture to the margarine mixture, and process to mix well. Fold in the carrots and raisins.

3 Coat an 8-inch square pan with nonstick cooking spray. Pat the mixture evenly in the pan, and bake at 350°F for 25 to 30 minutes, or until a wooden toothpick inserted in the center comes out clean. Cool to room temperature, cut into squares, and serve.

RASPBERRY APPLE TURNOVERS

Yield: 12 turnovers

Filling:

1 tablespoon cornstarch

3 tablespoons apple juice

1-1/4 cups finely chopped fresh apples (about 2 medium)

1/4 cup golden raisins

2 tablespoons sugar

1/2 cup fresh or frozen raspberries

Pastry:

1-1/4 cups unbleached flour

1 cup oat bran

2 tablespoons sugar

1/2 teaspoon baking powder

4 tablespoons chilled reduced-fat margarine or light butter, cut into pieces

1/2 cup plus 2 tablespoons nonfat buttermilk

Glaze:

1 tablespoon beaten egg white

1 tablespoon water

1 tablespoon sugar

To make the filling, combine the cornstarch and 1 tablespoon of the apple juice, and set aside. Combine the remaining apple juice, apples, raisins, and sugar in a small saucepan. Cover, and cook over medium-low heat for 5 to 7 minutes, stirring occasionally, until the apples are tender. Stir in the raspberries, and cook uncovered for another minute or 2, until the raspberries are soft and begin to break up. Stir in the cornstarch mixture, and cook for another minute or 2, stirring constantly, until the mixture is thickened and bubbly. Remove from the heat and set aside to cool.

2. To make the pastry, combine the flour, oat bran, sugar, and baking powder, and stir to mix well. Use a pastry cutter to cut in the margarine or butter until the mixture resembles coarse crumbs. Stir in just enough of the buttermilk to make a stiff dough that leaves the sides of the bowl and forms a ball.

3. Turn the dough onto a generously floured surface, and divide into 2 pieces. Use a rolling pin to roll each piece into an 8-x-12-inch rectangle. Use a knife or pizza wheel to cut each rectangle into six 4-inch squares.

4. Place a slightly rounded tablespoon of filling in the center of each square. Bring one corner over the filling and match up with the opposite corner to form a triangle. Seal the turnovers by crimping the edges with the tines of a fork. Dip the fork in sugar to prevent sticking if necessary

5. Coat a baking sheet with nonstick cooking spray. Lift the turnovers with a spatula and transfer to the baking sheet. Combine the egg white and water, and brush over the tops of the pastries. Sprinkle 1/4 teaspoon of sugar over each turnover.

6. Bake at 375°F for 20 minutes, or until the edges are lightly browned. Transfer to a serving platter, and serve warm.

HAMANTASCHEN

Yield: *40 pastries*

NUTRITIONAL FACTS (PER PASTRY)
CALORIES: 53
FAT: 0.8 G
PROTEIN: 1.4 G
CHOLESTEROL: 0 MG
SODIUM: 35 MG
FIBER: 0.8 G
CALCIUM: 6 MG
POTASSIUM: 69 MG
IRON: 0.5 MG

These fruit-filled treats are traditionally served on the Jewish holiday Purim.

Filling:

1 cup finely chopped dried apricots, prunes, or other dried fruit

1 cup water

2 tablespoons honey

Pastry:

5 tablespoons reduced-fat margarine or light butter

1/4 cup plus 2 tablespoons sugar

3 egg whites

1-1/4 cups whole wheat flour

1-1/4 cups unbleached flour

1-1/2 teaspoons baking powder

Glaze:

2 tablespoons beaten egg white

1 teaspoon water

Sugar (optional)

1 To make the glaze, combine the egg white and water, mixing well. Set aside.

2 To make the filling, combine the apricots, water, and honey in a small saucepan, and bring to a boil over high heat. Reduce the heat to low, cover, and simmer for about 20 minutes, stirring occasionally, until the liquid is absorbed. Remove from the heat and cool to room temperature.

3 Combine the margarine or butter and the sugar in the bowl of an electric mixer, and beat until smooth. Add the egg whites, and beat until smooth. In a separate bowl, combine the flours and baking powder, and stir to mix well. Add the flour mixture to the margarine mixture, and beat until the dough leaves the sides of the bowl and forms a ball.

4 Place 1/4 of the dough on a floured surface, leaving the remaining dough covered to prevent it from drying out. Roll the dough out to 1/16-inch thickness, and use a 3-inch glass or cookie cutter to cut rounds out of the dough. (If the dough is too sticky to handle, place it in the freezer for a few minutes.)

5 Brush a small amount of glaze around the outer edges of each circle. Place 1 teaspoon of filling in the center of each round, and fold up 3 sides of each circle about 1/2 inch to form a tricorn—a 3-sided hat. Note that the filling should not be totally covered by the pastry. Pinch the corners together so that the edges remain up.

6 Coat a baking sheet with nonstick cooking spray, and transfer the pastries to the sheet. Brush some glaze over each pastry, and lightly sprinkle with sugar if desired. Bake at 325°F for about 20 minutes, or until golden brown. Transfer to wire racks, and cool completely before serving.

PINEAPPLE ALMOND BARS

Yield: 16 servings

| NUTRITIONAL FACTS |
(PER SERVING)
CALORIES: 100
FAT: 2.3 G
PROTEIN: 1.5 G
CHOLESTEROL: 0 MG
SODIUM: 73 MG
FIBER: 0.7 G
CALCIUM: 11 MG
POTASSIUM: 51 MG
IRON: 0.8 MG

For variety, make these delicious bars with raspberry or apricot preserves.

3/4 cup unbleached flour

3/4 cup quick-cooking oats

1/4 cup plus 2 tablespoons light brown sugar

1/2 teaspoon baking soda

5 tablespoons reduced-fat margarine or light butter, cut into pieces

1 teaspoon almond extract

2 tablespoons sliced almonds

1/2 cup pineapple preserves

1 Place the flour, oats, brown sugar, and baking soda in the bowl of a food processor, and process for a few seconds to mix well. Add the margarine or butter and the almond extract, and process until crumbly.

2 Remove 1/2 cup of the crumbs, and mix with the almonds. Set aside.

3 Coat an 8-inch square pan with nonstick cooking spray. Pat the plain crumb mixture into an even layer on the bottom of the pan. Spread the preserves in a layer over the crust, extending the filling to within 1/4 inch of each edge. Sprinkle the crumb-almond mixture over the preserves.

4 Bake at 350°F for 30 minutes, or until browned and crisp. Cool to room temperature, cut into squares, and serve.

LIGHT AND LUSCIOUS BROWNIES

Yield: 16 servings

NUTRITIONAL FACTS (PER SERVING)
CALORIES: 95
FAT: 2.4 G
PROTEIN: 1.6 G
CHOLESTEROL: 0 MG
SODIUM: 74 MG
FIBER: 0.7 G
CALCIUM: 4 MG
POTASSIUM: 29 MG
IRON: 0.5 MG

6 tablespoons reduced-fat margarine or light butter
1 cup sugar
3 egg whites
1 teaspoon vanilla extract
3/4 cup unbleached flour
1/3 cup cocoa powder
1/3 cup chopped nuts (optional)

1 Place the margarine or butter in a medium-sized saucepan, and melt over low heat. Remove the pan from the heat, and stir in first the sugar, and then the egg whites and vanilla extract. Stir in the flour and cocoa powder. Fold in the nuts if desired.

2 Coat an 8-inch square pan with nonstick cooking spray. Spread the batter evenly in the pan, and bake at 325°F for about 25 minutes, or until the edges are firm and the center is almost set. Cool to room temperature, cut into squares, and serve.

ALMOND BISCOTTI

Yield: 24 biscotti

NUTRITIONAL FACTS
(PER BISCOTTI)

CALORIES: 76

FAT: 1.8 G

PROTEIN: 1.9 G

CHOLESTEROL: 0 MG

SODIUM: 57 MG

FIBER: 1 G

CALCIUM: 12 MG

POTASSIUM: 43 MG

IRON: 0.5 MG

1 cup unbleached flour

1 cup whole wheat flour

2/3 cup sugar

2 teaspoons baking powder

4 tablespoons reduced-fat margarine
   or light butter

3 egg whites

1 teaspoon vanilla extract

1 teaspoon almond extract

1/4 cup finely chopped almonds

1 Combine the flours, sugar, and baking powder, and stir to mix well. Use a pastry cutter to cut in the margarine or butter until the mixture resembles coarse meal. Stir in the egg whites and the vanilla and almond extracts. Fold in the almonds.

2 Turn the dough onto a lightly floured surface, and shape into two 9-x-2-inch logs. Coat a baking sheet with nonstick cooking spray, and place the logs on the sheet, leaving 4 inches of space between the logs to allow for spreading. Bake at 350°F for about 25 minutes, or until lightly browned.

3 Cool the logs at room temperature for 10 minutes. Then use a serrated knife to slice the logs diagonally into 1/2-inch-thick slices.

4 Place the slices on an ungreased baking sheet in a single layer, cut side down. Bake at 350°F for 18 to 20 minutes, or until dry and crisp, turning the slices over after 10 minutes.

5 Transfer the biscotti to wire racks, and cool completely. Serve immediately or store in an airtight container.

WHOLE WHEAT CHOCOLATE CHIPPERS

Yield: 40 cookies

NUTRITIONAL FACTS
(PER COOKIE)

CALORIES: 50	
FAT: 1.6 G	
PROTEIN: 0.8 G	
CHOLESTEROL: 0 MG	
SODIUM: 41 MG	
FIBER: 0.5 G	
CALCIUM: 6 MG	
POTASSIUM: 42 MG	
IRON: 0.4 MG	

6 tablespoons reduced-fat margarine
    or light butter
3/4 cup light brown sugar
3 tablespoons fat-free egg substitute
1 teaspoon vanilla extract
1-1/4 cups whole wheat flour
1/2 teaspoon baking soda
1/2 cup chocolate chips
1/3 cup Grape-Nuts cereal or chopped
    walnuts

1 Combine the margarine or butter, brown sugar, egg substitute, and vanilla extract in the bowl of a food processor or electric mixer, and process until smooth. In a separate bowl, combine the flour and baking soda. Add the flour mixture to the margarine mixture, and process to mix well. Stir in the remaining ingredients.

2 Coat a baking sheet with nonstick cooking spray. Drop rounded teaspoonfuls of dough onto the baking sheet, placing them 1-1/2 inches apart.

3 Bake at 300°F for about 16 minutes, or until golden brown. Cool the cookies on the pan for 1 minute. Then transfer the cookies to wire racks, and cool completely. Serve immediately, or transfer to an airtight container.

BUTTERSCOTCH CRISPS

Yield: 40 cookies

NUTRITIONAL FACTS
(PER COOKIE)

CALORIES: 52
FAT: 1.6 G
PROTEIN: 1 G
CHOLESTEROL: 0 MG
SODIUM: 48 MG
FIBER: 0.7 G
CALCIUM: 5 MG
POTASSIUM: 44 MG
IRON: 0.4 MG

6 tablespoons reduced-fat margarine
    or light butter

1/2 cup plus 2 tablespoons sugar

3 tablespoons fat-free egg substitute

1 tablespoon molasses

1 teaspoon vanilla extract

1-1/4 cups whole wheat flour

1/2 teaspoon baking soda

1/2 cup butterscotch chips

2/3 cup Grape-Nuts cereal

1 Combine the margarine or butter, sugar, egg substitute, molasses, and vanilla extract in the bowl of a food processor or electric mixer, and process until smooth. In a separate bowl, combine the flour and baking soda. Add the flour mixture to the margarine mixture, and process to mix well. Stir in the remaining ingredients.

2 Coat a baking sheet with nonstick cooking spray. Drop rounded teaspoonfuls of dough onto the baking sheet, placing them 1-1/2 inches apart.

3 Bake at 300°F for about 16 minutes, or until golden brown. Cool the cookies on the pan for 1 minute. Then transfer the cookies to wire racks, and cool completely. Serve immediately, or transfer to an airtight container.

GREAT GRANOLA COOKIES

Yield: 36 cookies

6 tablespoons reduced-fat margarine or light butter

3/4 cup light brown sugar

3 tablespoons fat-free egg substitute

1 teaspoon vanilla extract

1/2 cup plus 2 tablespoons whole wheat flour

1/2 cup unbleached flour

1/2 teaspoon baking soda

1 cup nonfat or low-fat granola cereal

1/2 cup chopped dried apricots

1/4 cup hulled sunflower seeds or chopped nuts (optional)

1 Combine the margarine, brown sugar, egg substitute, and vanilla extract in the bowl of a food processor or electric mixer, and process to mix well. In a mixing bowl, combine the flours and baking soda. Add the flour mixture to the margarine mixture, and process to mix well. Stir in the remaining ingredients.

2 Coat a baking sheet with nonstick cooking spray. Drop slightly rounded teaspoonfuls of dough onto the baking sheet, placing them 1-1/2 inches apart. Flatten each cookie slightly with the tip of a spoon.

3 Bake at 300°F for about 15 minutes, or until golden brown. Cool the cookies on the pan for 1 minute. Then transfer the cookies to wire racks, and cool completely. Serve immediately, or transfer to an airtight container.

ULTIMATE OATMEAL COOKIES

Yield: 42 cookies

NUTRITIONAL FACTS (PER COOKIE)
CALORIES: 45
FAT: 0.9 G
PROTEIN: 0.9 G
CHOLESTEROL: 0 MG
SODIUM: 31 MG
FIBER: 0.7 G
CALCIUM: 6 MG
POTASSIUM: 41 MG
IRON: 0.3 MG

6 tablespoons reduced-fat margarine or light butter

3/4 cup light brown sugar

3 tablespoons fat-free egg substitute

1 teaspoon vanilla extract

1 cup whole wheat flour

1 cup quick-cooking oats

1/2 teaspoon baking soda

1/2 cup dark raisins, chopped dried apricots, or other chopped dried fruit

1/4 cup chopped walnuts, pecans, or almonds (optional)

1 Combine the margarine or butter, brown sugar, egg substitute, and vanilla extract in the bowl of a food processor or electric mixer, and process until smooth. In a separate bowl, combine the flour, oats, and baking soda. Add the flour mixture to the margarine mixture, and process to mix well. Stir in the remaining ingredients.

2 Coat a baking sheet with nonstick cooking spray. Drop rounded tea-spoonfuls of dough onto the baking sheet, placing them 1-1/2 inches apart. Flatten each cookie slightly with the tip of a spoon.

3 Bake at 300°F for 15 to 18 minutes, or until lightly browned and crisp. Cool the cookies on the pan for 1 minute. Then transfer the cookies to wire racks, and cool completely. Serve immediately, or transfer to an airtight container.

THUMBPRINT COOKIES

Yield: 36 cookies

NUTRITIONAL FACTS (PER COOKIE)
CALORIES: 44
FAT: 0.8 G
PROTEIN: 0.8 G
CHOLESTEROL: 0 MG
SODIUM: 33 MG
FIBER: 0.5 G
CALCIUM: 3 MG
POTASSIUM: 27 MG
IRON: 0.3 MG

4 tablespoons reduced-fat margarine or light butter

1/2 cup plus 2 tablespoons sugar

3 tablespoons frozen orange juice concentrate, thawed

1 teaspoon vanilla or almond extract

1 cup plus 2 tablespoons unbleached flour

3/4 cup oat bran

3/4 teaspoon baking soda

1/3 cup finely ground nuts (optional)

3 tablespoons fruit spread or jam, any flavor

1 Combine the margarine or butter and the sugar in the bowl of a food processor or electric mixer, and process until smooth. Add the juice concentrate and vanilla or almond extract, and process until smooth. In a separate bowl, combine the flour, oat bran, and baking soda. Add the flour mixture to the margarine mixture, and process until the dough leaves the sides of the bowl and forms a ball.

2 Coat a baking sheet with nonstick cooking spray. Roll the dough into 1-inch balls. (If the dough is too sticky to handle, place it in the freezer for a few minutes.) Roll the balls in the nuts if desired, and place them on the sheet, spacing them 1-1/2 inches apart. Using the back of a 1/4-teaspoon measuring spoon, make a depression in the center of each ball. (Dip the spoon in sugar, if necessary, to prevent sticking.) Fill each depression with 1/4 teaspoon of jam.

3 Bake at 300°F for 18 to 20 minutes. To check for doneness, lift a cookie from the sheet with a spatula. The bottom should be golden brown. Cool the cookies on the pan for 1 minute. Then transfer the cookies to wire racks, and cool completely. Serve immediately, or transfer to an airtight container.

CHOCOLATE RASPBERRY TREATS

Yield: 42 cookies

NUTRITIONAL FACTS
(PER COOKIE)

CALORIES: 50	
FAT: 0.8 G	
PROTEIN: 1 G	
CHOLESTEROL: 0 MG	
SODIUM: 33 MG	
FIBER: 0.9 G	
CALCIUM: 7 MG	
POTASSIUM: 45 MG	
IRON: 0.5 MG	

4 tablespoons reduced-fat margarine
   or light butter

3/4 cup light brown sugar

1/4 cup chocolate syrup

1 tablespoon plus 1 teaspoon water

1 teaspoon vanilla extract

1-1/2 cups whole wheat flour

1 cup quick-cooking oats

2 tablespoons cocoa powder

3/4 teaspoon baking soda

3 tablespoons plus 1-1/2 teaspoons
   raspberry fruit spread or jam

1 Combine the margarine or butter and the brown sugar in the bowl of a food processor or electric mixer, and process until smooth. Add the chocolate syrup, water, and vanilla extract, and process until smooth. In a separate bowl, combine the flour, oats, cocoa, and baking soda. Add the flour mixture to the margarine mixture, and process until the dough leaves the sides of the bowl and forms a ball.

2 Coat a baking sheet with nonstick cooking spray. Roll the dough into 1-inch balls, and place the balls on the sheet, spacing them 1-1/2 inches apart. (If the dough is too sticky to handle, place it in the freezer for a few minutes.) Using the back of a 1/4-teaspoon measuring spoon, make a depression in the center of each ball. (Dip the spoon in sugar, if necessary, to prevent sticking.) Fill each depression with 1/4 teaspoon of jam.

3 Bake at 300°F for 18 to 20 minutes. To check for doneness, lift a cookie from the sheet with a spatula. The bottom should be nicely browned. Cool the cookies on the pan for 1 minute. Then transfer the cookies to wire racks, and cool completely. Serve immediately, or transfer to an airtight container.

ost of the ingredients used in the recipes in this book are readily available in any supermarket, or can be found in your local health foods store or gourmet shop. But if you are unable to locate what you're looking for, the following list should guide you to a manufacturer who can either sell the desired product to you directly or inform you of the nearest retail outlet.

Whole Grains and Flours

Arrowhead Mills, Inc.
Box 2059
Hereford, TX 79045
(800) 749-0730

Whole wheat pastry flour, oat flour, and other flours and whole grains.

King Arthur Flour
PO Box 876
Norwich, VT 05055
(800) 827-6836

White whole wheat flour and other flours, whole grains, and baking products.

Mountain Ark Trading Company
PO Box 3170
Fayetteville, AR 72702
(800) 643-8909

Whole grains and flours, unrefined sweeteners, dried fruits, fruit spreads, and a wide variety of other natural foods.

Walnut Acres
Walnut Acres Road
Penns Creek, PA 17862
(800) 433-3998 (717) 837-0601

Baking and cooking aids, whole grains and flours, unrefined sweeteners, dried fruits, and a wide variety of other natural foods.

Sweeteners

Fruit Source
1803 Mission Street, Suite 401
Santa Cruz, CA 95060
(408) 457-1136

Fruit Source granulated and liquid sweeteners.

Lundberg Family Farms
PO Box 369
Richvale, CA 95974-0369
(916) 882-4551

Brown rice syrup.

NutraCane, Inc.
5 Meadowbrook Parkway
Milford, NH 03055
(603) 672-2801

Sucanat granulated sweetener.

Vermont Country Maple, Inc.
PO Box 53
Jericho Center, VT 05465
(800) 528-7021

Maple sugar, maple syrup, and other maple products.

Westbrae Natural Foods
1065 East Walnut
Carson, CA 90746
(310) 886-8200

Brown rice syrup.